Hello and welcome!

Dein *Wordmaster-Heft* hilft dir beim Wörterlernen.

In der Schule lernst du Englisch mit dem Buch *Go Ahead 8*. Dort besprecht ihr auch die neuen Wörter einer Seite.

Danach machst du zuerst die Übung **New words** in deinem *Wordmaster-Heft*, die zu der neuen Seite in deinem Englischbuch gehört. Bei dieser Aufgabe fügst du die neuen Wörter zum Beispiel in einen Text oder einen Dialog ein, oder du ordnest ihnen Definitionen zu. So übst du die neuen Wörter auf vielfältige Weise.

Wenn du einmal nicht weiterweißt, darfst du im *Unit-Vocabulary* (Wörterverzeichnis) von *Go Ahead 8* (S. 178–210) nachschauen.

Anschließend kannst du überprüfen, ob du alles richtig gelöst hast: Die Lösungen findest du im eingehefteten Lösungsteil.

Wenn du sicher bist, dass die Lösung richtig ist, präge dir die Sätze und Worterklärungen ein. So behältst du die neuen Wörter besser!

Nach **New words** bietet der *Wordmaster* noch weitere Übungen zum Lernen der neuen Wörter, zum Beispiel Wortspiele und Rätsel.

Am Ende jeder *Wordmaster-Unit* findest du dein **Learner log**, dein Lerntagebuch. Dort kannst du Fragen zu deinen Erfahrungen mit dem Wörterlernen beantworten.

Damit du überprüfen kannst, wie gut du die Wörter aus den vorigen Units noch beherrschst, gibt es an drei Stellen im *Wordmaster-Heft Revision*-Aufgaben: Nach Unit 2 überprüfen sie den Wortschatz der ersten beiden Units, nach Unit 4 den Wortschatz von Unit 3 und 4 und nach Unit 5 Wörter aus dem Gesamtwortschatz von *Go Ahead 8*.

Viel Spaß beim Englischlernen!

The USA: facts and figures

1 New words SB pp. 8–9

Read what Juan and Lara tell the class and write the English words in the gaps.

As you all know, the USA is a very big country: the total area is 9,629,091 **1** ______________ *(Quadratkilometer)*. The first immigrants who came here wanted to leave their old identities behind and become "Americans", which is why people often called the USA a **2** ______________ *(Schmelztiegel)*. Today many people believe that immigrants want to keep their **3** ______________ *(kulturelle)* identities. The history of the USA began when 13 states **4** ______________ *(sich trennten)* from Great Britain. The thirteen **5** ______________ in today's American flag are for them.

As an exchange student from Germany, getting used to American **6** ______________ *(alltäglich)* life isn't always easy for me. I have the **7** ______________ *(Eindruck)* that you do some things quite differently here in the **8** ______________ *(Mittlerer Westen)*. But the biggest difference is the American **9** ______________ *(Maßeinheiten)*. We measure distance in kilometres, you use **10** ______________. We measure **11** ______________ *(Volumen)* in **12** ______________, you use **13** ______________. The most difficult thing for me is talking about temperature. I know that 30 **14** ______________ *(Grad)* Celsius is hot, but how much is that in **15** ______________?

The American dream

Unit **1**

1 New words SB *pp. 10–11*

Read the sentences and complete them with the words from the box.

achieved • African American • ancestors • check in • definition • huddled • Liberty • masses • perform • personal • yearned for • yearned to

Our flight to New York City was delayed. So we called the hotel from the airport to ask the receptionist how late we could **1** ______________. She said it was no problem because they allowed 24-hour check-in.

We went to see the Statue of **2** ______________ and Ellis Island on our trip to New York.

We bought tickets for our visit online because in our guide it said there are usually **3** ______________ of people waiting to go to Liberty Island and Ellis Island.

The ferry was late, and it was very cold outside. So we **4** ______________ together to keep warm until the ferry arrived.

Today, we're going to talk about the American Dream. Let's find a good **5** ______________ first. Then I'd like you to give some examples from your family history or your **6** ______________ experience.

I'm **7** ______________.

My **8** ______________ came to America as slaves.

They **9** ______________ freedom.

My dad came to America from Iran because he **10** ______________ become a writer, but it was too dangerous there. He worked hard and **11** ______________ a lot.

I'm going to **12** ______________ in a play this year. I'll play an old woman who came to the USA through Ellis Island as a young girl and settled in California.

2 New words SB pp. 12–13

Write the English words in the gaps.

Mom, can you please help me to

1 __________ *(interpretieren)* the

2 __________ *(Liedtext)* of this Beastie Boys song?

Yes, of course. There's the Bronx in the north, then Manhattan, Queens, Brooklyn and Staten Island in the south.

Do you know the five

3 __________ *(Stadtbezirke)* of New York City?

And can you tell me the best

4 __________ *(Weg)* from the Bronx to Brooklyn?

Is there a **5** __________ *(U-Bahn)*?

In America liberty means the **6** __________ *(Freiheit)* to be who you want to be.

How was your Dad's

7 __________ *(Gefühls-zustand)* when you visited him in hospital?

Not very good. He is worried about our

8 __________ *(finanzielle)* situation.

3 New words *SB pp. 14–15*

Write the missing words in the crossword.

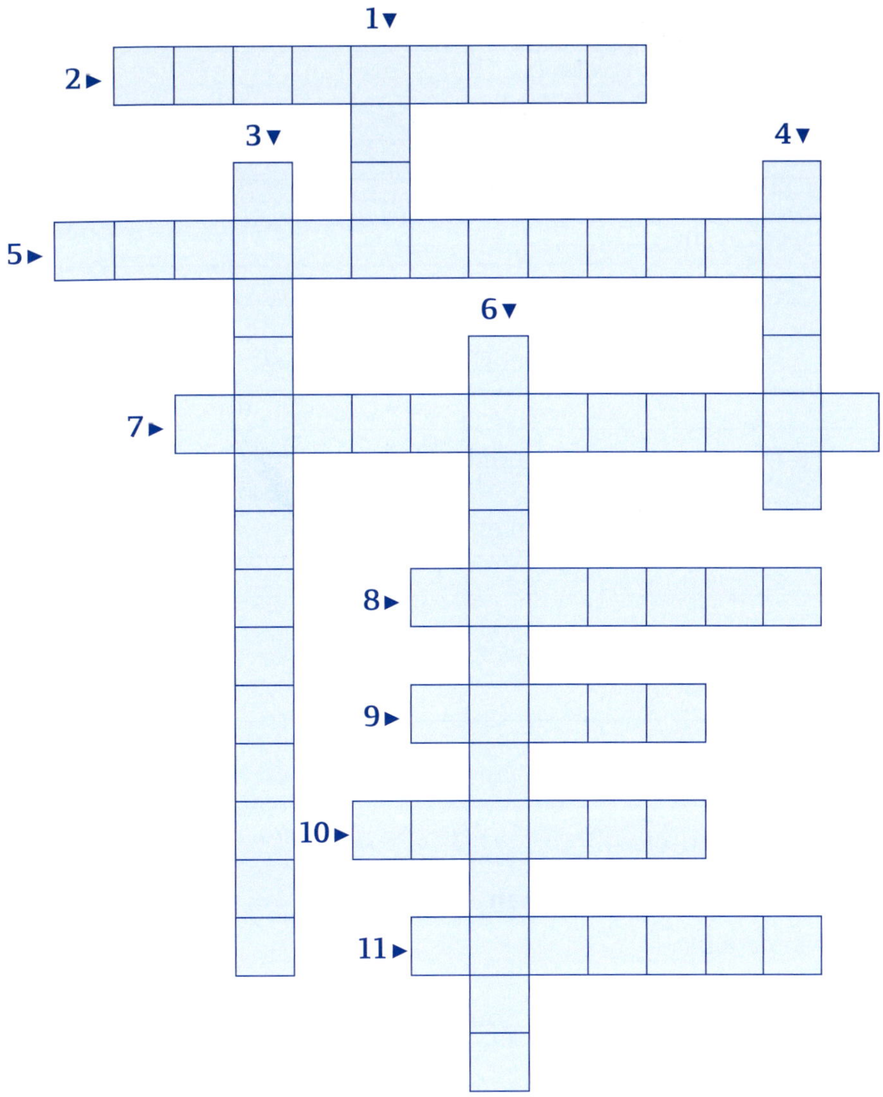

1 what you pay to live in a flat that you don't own
2 My dad needs some very expensive medicine, but his health ??? pays for it.
3 adjective: responsible – noun: ???
4 We use some English words in German. But often the ??? is different.
5 information in a newspaper, etc. that tells you about a job or something you can buy
6 the part of a town around where you live (*BE*)
7 the state of not having a place to live
8 a safe place where homeless people can spend the night
9

10 a time, usually at night, where people mustn't be or go outside
11 You were born in New York City. Is that ??? ?

4 Word families

Use the word given in capitals at the end of each line to form another word of the same word family that fits in the sentence in the same line.

1 *Freedom* ______ is the right of choice.	FREE
2 Please show your passport at the ______.	CHECK IN
3 ______ is a big problem in most towns and cities.	HOMELESS
4 Thirty years ago only a few people owned mobile phones. Today there is a ______ market for them.	MASSES
5 The next ______ of our show starts at 5 pm.	PERFORM
6 May I ask you a ______ question?	PERSON

5 Verbs and nouns and what they mean in German

a) Write the missing words in the table.

	verb	in German	noun	in German
1	(to) rent			
2			advertisement	
3				Betonung
4				Errungenschaft, Leistung

b) Now complete the sentences with a suitable word from the table in a).

1 I want to sell my car. I think I'll ______ it in our newspaper.

2 Where is the ______ in the word "modern"?

3 Getting a job as a doctor has been her biggest ______ so far.

4 We moved to a smaller flat because we couldn't afford the ______ any more.

6 New words SB p. 16

Complete the dialogue with the words from the box.

addict • applicants • apply for • citizenship • committed • enter • expiration • harm • issue • property

Grandad: Thanks, Dan, for helping me to fill in this application form.

Dan: No problem, Grandad. I did it with Mum last year, so I know what

1 ____________________ need to do.
Let's start at the top.
In the first box you have to

2 ____________________ your family name.

Grandad: Right. Date and city of birth are easy too.

Dan: Oh, I didn't know that you were born in Germany. What's your country of

3 ____________________ then?

Grandad: Great Britain. I came here as a boy. My parents had some **4** ____________________ in London, so it was easy for us to become British.

Dan: I see. Now when did you get your passport? What's the date of **5** ____________________?

Grandad: Let me see. That's 5th May 2010.

Dan: Okay! And what's the date of **6** ____________________ of your passport?

Grandad: Oh no, my passport expired on 4th May. So I have to **7** ____________________ a new one. What do we do now?

Dan: We can answer the questions at the bottom, save the information and complete the application form when you have your new passport. Question number one:

Are you a drug **8** ____________________?

Grandad: Oh no, I've never taken any drugs!

Dan: OK. Have you ever **9** ____________________ a crime?

Grandad: Of course not. I would never do any **10** ____________________ to anybody!

Dan: I know, Grandad.

7 New words SB p. 17

Complete Kelly's email with the words from the box.

bill • booked • change • closets • coffee • fare • first floor • key card • receptionist • tip • traffic • vending machine • waiters and waitresses

Dear Mom and Dad,

I hope you're fine. I'm writing to you from my hotel room. You **1** ________________ the right place for me! My room is on the **2** ____________________, but the hotel is in a side street, so there isn't a lot of **3** ________________.

There's a safe in one of the **4** ___________________ where I can keep my passport and my money! I'm glad I brought enough **5** ___________________. I needed it for the bus **6** ___________________ from the airport to the hotel, and there is a **7** ________________ ___________________ at the hotel. I've just bought a nice cup of **8** ________________ from it.

The people I've met so far have been really friendly. The **9** __________________________ showed me how to use the **10** ___________________ for my room. The **11** ____________ __________________________ in the hotel restaurant are very nice too. Do you know if I have to give them a **12** ________________ every day, or is it OK if I add some money to the **13** ________________ at the end of my stay?

Lots of love, Kelly

8 American English – British English

Write the missing words in American or British English and their German meaning.

	American English	British English	in German
1		underground	U-
2	neighborhood		
3	first floor		
4		second floor	
5	second floor		
6	expiration		
7		wardrobe/cupboard	

9 New words SB pp. 18–21

Write the missing words in the crossword.

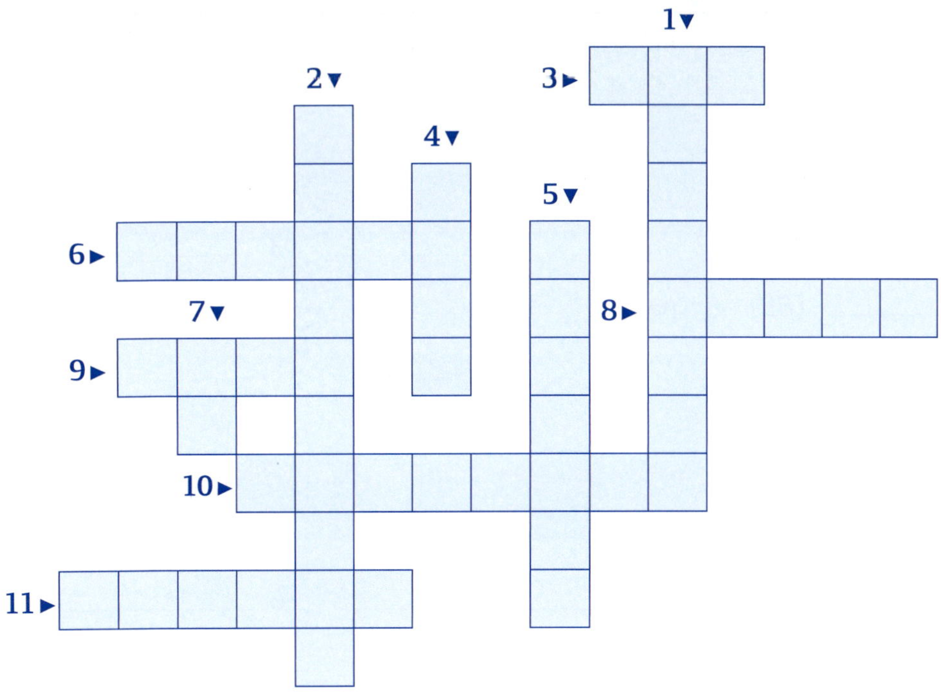

1 The ??? of big is small.
2 Their car is in terrible ??? after their accident.
3 ◄► high
4 Lots of roads ??? to New York City.
5 a yellow sauce that you put on a sausage, for example
6 a street, often with trees
7 You write ???, you say "for example".
8 
9 a shop that sells special food
10 a name that your friends or family call you, but which isn't your real name
11 Please don't check your phone ??? the lesson!

10 How to say it

*Where is the stress in the words in **bold**? Circle the part of the word that you stress when you say it.*

1 Do you know where your **ancestors** came from?

2 Can you give me a **definition** of freedom?

3 My uncle never had **financial** problems.

4 Sometimes we have to **interpret** poems in our English class.

5 Many American teenagers have a 10 pm **curfew**.

6 Do you have travel **insurance**?

7 What is the **volume** of your backpack?

11 New words SB p. 22

a) Write the English words under the pictures.

1 ______________________ (AE) 2 an ______________________ 3 ______________________

______________________ (BE) person jeans

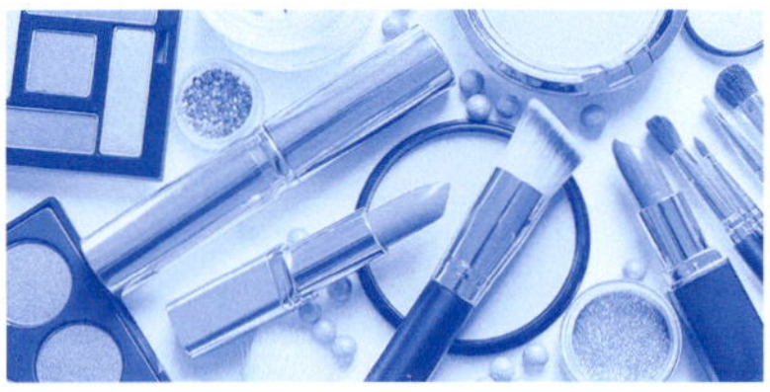
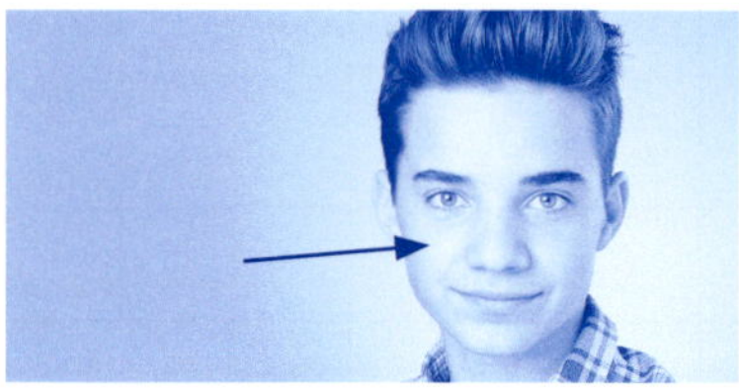
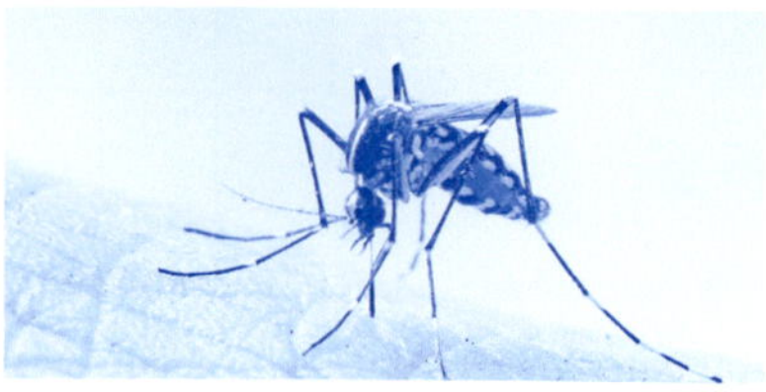

4 ______________________ 5 ______________________ 6 ______________________

b) Complete the sentences with the words from the box.

acted • as soon as • manicure • promise • professional • résumé • schedule • vibrated

1 Evie's cell phone ______________________ and she took the call.

2 "Can you come to my party?" – "I'll let you know ______________________ possible."

3 John wants to become a ______________________ football player and earn a lot of money.

4 Sam ______________________ very quickly after the accident and called the police.

5 "Mum, can you please help me write my ______________________." – "I'll try to, but I can't ______________________. I have a very tight ______________________ this week."

6 "My hands look terrible! I need to get a ______________________ soon.

c) Match the words with the explanations.

1 all right
2 excellent
3 gel
4 demonstration
5 (to) nominate
6 cosmetics
7 fat

A things you use on your face to look more beautiful
B (to) suggest someone for a role or prize
C something you put on your hair or skin
D ◂▸ skinny
E OK
F showing how to do something
G very good

12 New words SB p. 23

a) Complete the dialogues with the words from the box.

a once-over • appreciate • heels • inches • sweating • take my eyes off • tight

Liz: Did you get the job?

Rod: No, the boss just gave me **1** ____________________ and walked away again.

Liz: How rude!

Holly: Mum, don't you think this dress is too **2** ____________________? Do I need a bigger size?

Mum: Oh no Dear! It looks so cute I can hardly **3** ____________________ you.

Dan: It's not fair, they don't **4** ____________________ us. We mowed the grass and cleaned up the garden!

Luc: I know! We're out here, **5** ____________________ in the sun, and they're off swimming in the pool!

Donna: These shoes have very high **6** ____________________.

Shop assistant: Yes, 6 cm. That about 2 1/2 **7** ____________________.

b) Write the English words under the pictures.

1 ____________________

2 ____________________

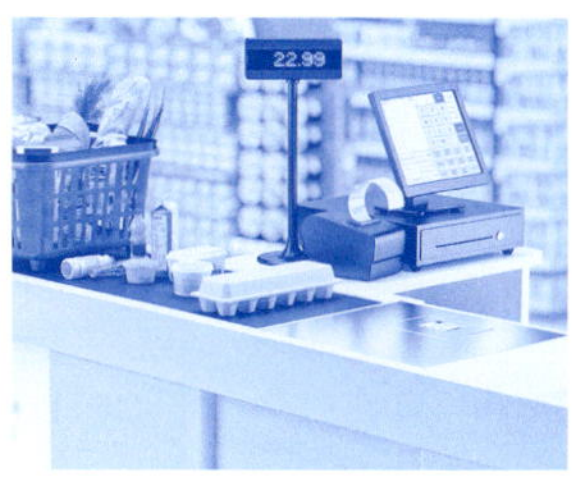

3 ____________________

4 ____________________

5 ______________ *(AE)*

______________ *(BE)*

6 ____________________

7 ____________________

____

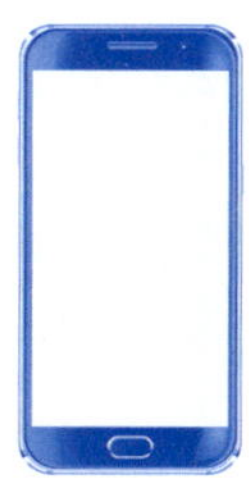

8 ______________ *(AE)*

______________ *(BE)*

13 New words SB p. 25

What do the following words mean? Match the expressions (A–G) with their corresponding definitions (1–7). Write the numbers in the grid below.

A (to) rhyme	**1** friendly towards visitors
B gritty	**2** a regular pattern of sounds in music
C pretty	**3** ►► very strong
D (to) collect	**4** when two words have the same sound at the end, they …
E rhythm	**5** (to) bring together similar things
F welcoming	**6** nice to look at
G extreme	**7** ►► showing something as it really is even if it isn't nice

A	B	C	D	E	F	G

14 American English – British English

Write the missing words in American or British English and their German meaning.

	American English	British English	in German
1		mobile (phone)	
2		shop	
3	restroom		
4	sidewalk		
5		holiday	
6		petrol station	
7	sneaker		
8		mum	

15 Opposites

Write the opposites.

1 (to) check in ◄► ______________________

2 high ◄► ______________________

3 baggy ◄► ______________________

4 rich ◄► ______________________

5 weak ◄► ______________________

6 long ◄► ______________________

16 Crossword

Write the missing words in the crossword.

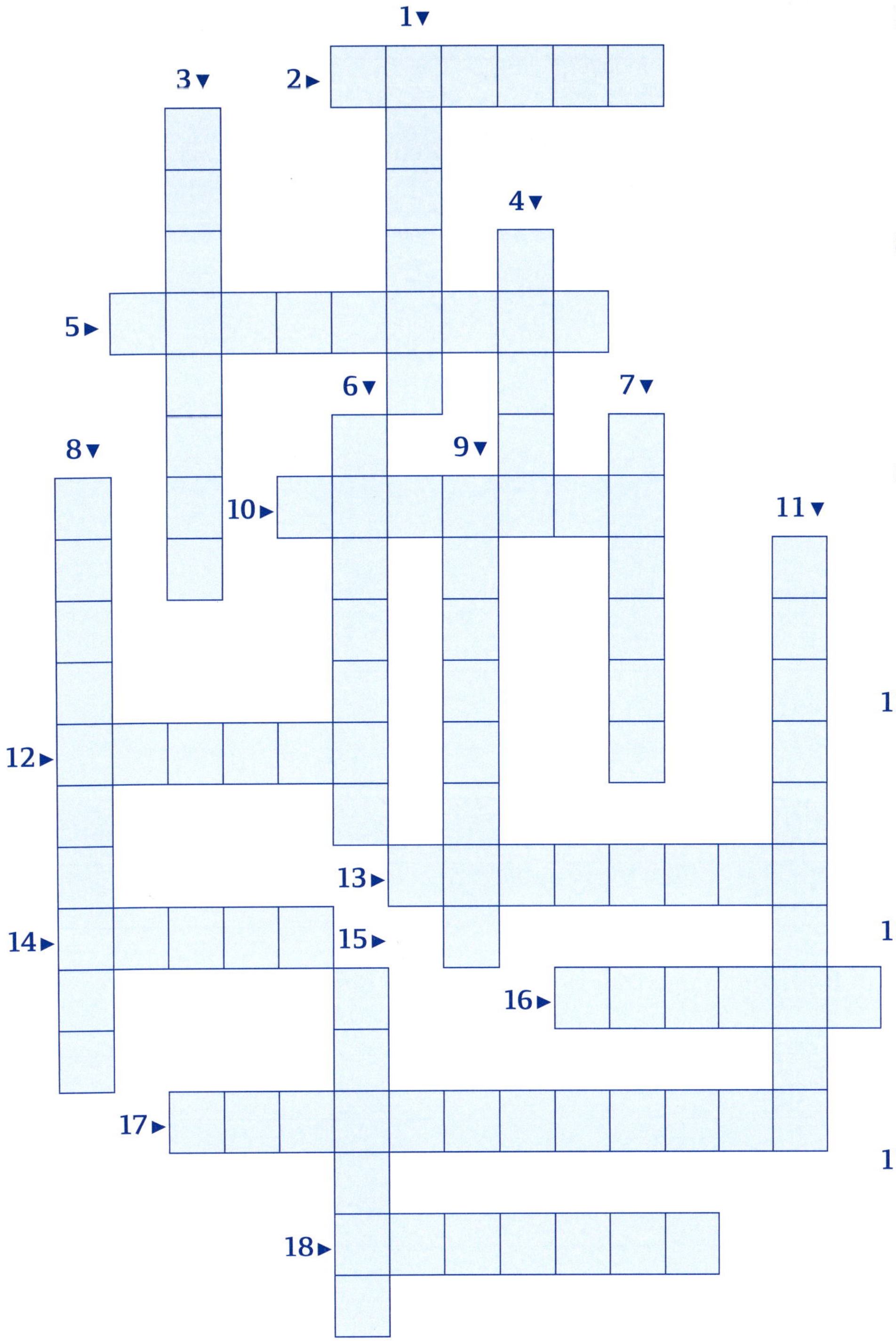

2

8

9

12

13

17

1 a person who can't stop doing or taking things that are bad for him or her
3 something you own
4 (to) fill in your name or other information into a form
5 somebody who applies for something
6 a person who belongs to a country or town
7 the words of a song
10 ►► freedom
11 when people are too heavy
14 when clothes are too small in size
15 nice to look at
16 money that you get back when you paid too much
18 all the cars, etc. that are on the road

17 Synonyms

Read the sentences and find the words in the box that has the same meaning as the underlined word in each sentence.

liberty • correct • great • store • mobile

1 Can I borrow your <u>cell</u>, please? I need to call my parents. ______________________

2 There's a good book <u>shop</u> in the city centre. ______________________

3 People often have to fight for their <u>freedom</u>. ______________________

4 We sell <u>excellent</u> food in our deli. ______________________

5 It's sometimes hard to find the <u>right</u> words. ______________________

My learner log

★ My three favourite words in this unit are:

____

I can …

- talk about the American dream *(Write one sentence about the American dream.)*:

____

____

- find pairs of British and American words *(Write two examples.)*:

____

____

What was difficult[1] in Unit 1:

____

What was easy in Unit 1:

____

What I liked about Unit 1:

____

[1] difficult *schwierig*

Land of the free?

Unit **2**

1 New words SB pp. 26–27

Read the definitions and write the words from the box next to them.

adobe • aspect • bead • braid • exhibition • feathers • headdress • indigenous (to) • jewellery • member • native • Native Americans • reservation • (to) search (for sth.) • stereotype • tribal elder

1 an area in the USA where only Native Americans live: ____________________

2 (to) look carefully because you are trying to find something: ____________________

3 one part of an idea or problem: ____________________

4 a hair style with long hair using three parts: ____________________

5 a group of things (e.g. very old objects or pieces of art) in one place so that people can look at them: ____________________

6 an important person, often an older person, in an Indian tribe: ____________________

7 a building material typical for hot areas: ____________________

8 a small ball of glass, plastic or wood with a hole in the middle: ____________________

9 things like rings or bracelets that you wear to look nice: ____________________

10 birds have lots of them on their bodies to keep them warm: ____________________

11 (to) be from the place where you were born: ____________________

12 another word for "native": ____________________

13 what people wear on their heads on special days: ____________________

14 "Girls don't like maths." – That's a ____________________

15 the people who lived in America before the Europeans arrived: ____________________

16 a person who is in a group or club: ____________________

2 New words SB pp. 28–29

Write the missing words in the crossword.

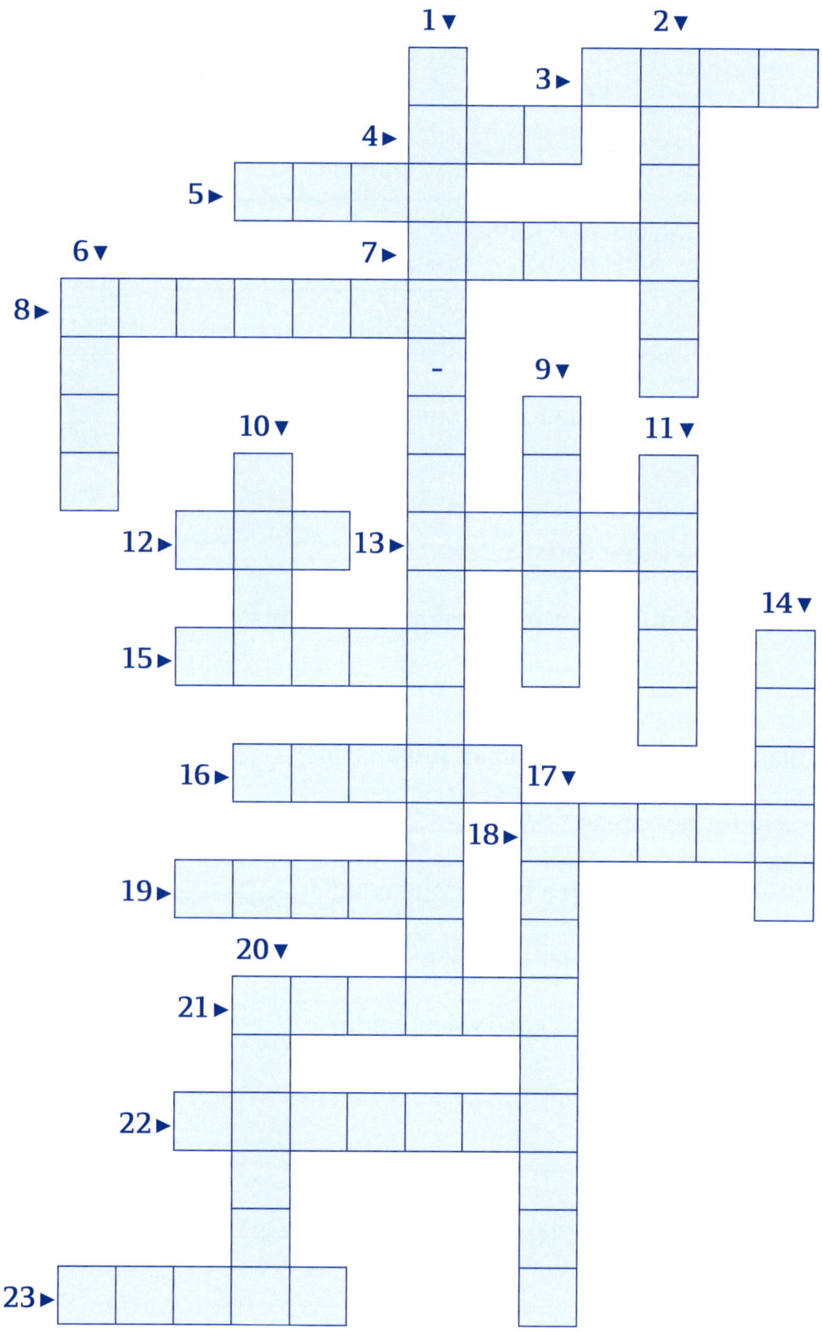

1 your grandmother's or grandfather's mother
2 (to) spread a disease (to sb.)
3 (to) pick something or somebody up
4 (to) move two things against each other
5

6 (to) put a dead body in the ground
7 ◄► below
8

9 a type of land that is wet
10 (to) bring something or somebody towards you
11 another word for "(to) start"

12 soft, wet earth
13 not sleeping
14 material we use to make clothes
15 When you cut your fingers, they ???.
16 
17 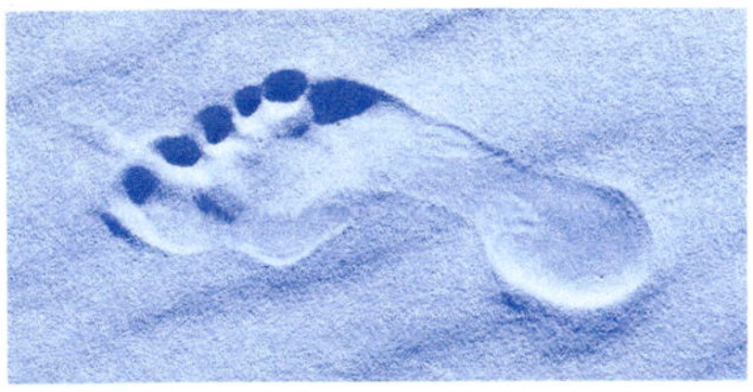
18 (to) move slowly in the air or on water
19 when someone puts their hand on you
20 
21 a person's mind, feelings and character; a ghost
22 
23 (to) move slowly on your hands and knees

3 Word families

Use the word given in capitals at the end of each line to form another word of the same word family that fits in the sentence in the same line.

1 Sam can't go swimming because he has a bad ear *infection* ______.	INFECT
2 Type your key words into a ______ engine.	SEARCH
3 "Women can't drive." and "Men never listen." These are stupid gender ______.	STEREOTYPICAL
4 Someone had hit him in the face, and now his nose was ______ badly.	BLOOD
5 Eric and Tim didn't like each other in the ______, but later they became good friends.	BEGIN
6 Please don't ______ these objects.	TOUCH
7 The apartment is on the 5th floor, and there is no ______. Going upstairs with heavy bags is no fun.	LIFT

4 New words SB pp. 30–31

Read the text and complete it with the words from the box.

alcohol • challenge • connect • difficult • driving licence *(BE)*/driver's license *(AE)* • dropped out • drunk driving • gun • minimum • poverty • unemployed

Clive has always had a hard life. He grew up in a neighbourhood where lots of people lived in **1** ______________________. Far too many people owned a **2** ______________________, and lots of people drank too much too. So **3** ______________________ was a big problem. Clive's father was a bus driver, but he often drank **4** ______________________.

He lost his **5** ______________________ and became **6** ______________________. Going to school and doing his homework was a big **7** ______________________ Clive faced every day. He **8** ______________________ of school and left home at the age of 15. After a few months he moved back home because he wanted to **9** ______________________ with his parents again. Clive went back to school too. Life is still **10** ______________________, but he has decided to become a bus driver, like his father, when he has reached the **11** ______________________ age for that job.

5 Prepositions

Complete the sentences with the right preposition.

for • on • out • through • to (2×)

1 There's something wrong here. My phone doesn't connect ______________ the Wi-Fi.

2 Lots of people search ______________ information on the internet these days.

3 Too many students drop ______________ of school at an early age.

4 Giraffes are indigenous ______________ Africa.

5 Feathers float ______________ water and ______________ the air.

6 New words SB p. 32

What do the following words mean? Match the expressions (A–I) with their corresponding definitions (1–11). Write the correct numbers in the grid below. Be careful: There are two definitions that you do not need.

- **A** bloodline
- **B** cattle
- **C** (to) be asleep
- **D** close-up
- **E** (to) fall asleep
- **F** long shot
- **G** medium shot
- **H** (to) shoot
- **I** wolf/wolves

1. a camera shot with only a little distance between the camera and the object
2. (to) go to sleep
3. a wild animal that looks a little like a dog
4. a person's or an animal's ancestors
5. a camera shot where you can see the object and a little of the background
6. (to) kill with a gun
7. a wild animal that looks a little like a cat
8. not awake
9. farm animals that we keep for their milk and meat
10. (to) go to bed
11. a camera shot where you can see the whole object and a lot of background

A	B	C	D	E	F	G	H	I

7 Odd word out

Circle the odd word out.

1. Native American – reservation – tribal elder – great-grandmother
2. panther – lion – cattle – cat
3. long shot – camera – close-up – medium shot
4. neighborhood – jewelry – subway – expiry
5. awake – poverty – difficult – unemployed

8 Opposites

Write the opposites.

1 above ◄► ______________________

2 easy ◄► ______________________

3 minimum ◄► ______________________

4 (to) end ◄► ______________________

9 New words SB p. 33

Use the pictures and the words in brackets to complete the sentences.

I'm a camera man. **1** ______________________ is very important for a good and **2** ______________________ *(inspirierend)* film. In older films the quality was sometimes quite **3** ______________________ *(minderwertig)*.

My **4** ______________________, my **5** ______________________ and I sometimes go camping together. The children love sitting around a **6** ______________________ listening to stories from the past.

My car is very old and **7** ______________________ very often. My sister has a **8** ______________________ *(fantastisch)* car, but I don't have enough money to buy one like that.

Some people leave **9** ______________________ *(gemein, fies)* comments on social media. I don't think that's very **10** ______________________ *(weise)* or **11** ______________________ *(respektvoll)*. It's just very stupid.

10 New words SB pp. 34–35

Complete the text with the words from the box. Use the correct form of the words.

chairperson • control • debate • guy • (to) increase • law • safety • suicide • (to) thank

Last night Jim watched a **1** ______________ on America's "gun culture" on TV. The **2** ______________ was a young news reporter from New York City. She said that according to US **3** ______________, Americans had the right to own a gun. An older man said that he had a gun for **4** ______________ reasons. A young **5** ______________ from California pointed out that guns weren't making the USA safer: he said that shootings and even **6** ______________ have **7** ______________ in the last few years. A teacher from Ohio said that she supported gun **8** ______________ because a lot of her students were scared of school shootings and felt very nervous at school. She **9** ______________ everybody who supported a ban on guns.

11 New words SB p. 36

What do the following words mean? Match the expressions (A–L) with their corresponding definitions (1–12). Write the correct numbers in the grid below.

A keyword
B engine
C quotation marks
D organization
E fake
F (to) bookmark
G (to) print sth. out
H (to) underline
I author
J less
K topic
L (to) refer to

1 someone who writes books
2 (to) put a line under a word or sentence
3 (to) talk about somebody or something
4 ◄► more
5 an important word, e.g. one you type into a search engine
6 a subject that you can research, talk or write about
7 the part of a car, train or plane that makes it work
8 symbols you use to show what somebody else has written or said
9 a group of people who work together to achieve a special aim
10 not real
11 when a machine produces words or pictures on a piece of paper
12 (to) mark a webpage or a page in a book that you want to go back to

A	B	C	D	E	F	G	H	I	J	K	L

12 New words SB p. 37

Complete the sentences with the words from the box. Use the right form of the words.

automatic • (to) pass • such a • such as

1 The Wounded Knee Massacre was ______________________ terrible event that I cried when I first read about it.

2 Joanna is very happy. She has just ______________________ her driving test.

3 If you're lucky you can see wild animals ______________________ wolves and black bears in New Mexico.

4 No to ______________________ weapons!

13 Verbs and nouns

Read the sentences. Some verbs and nouns are in the same form. Circle these nouns and underline these verbs.

1 My parents and their friends often debate about important things, but I didn't understand what last night's debate was about.

2 Students should respect their teachers, but teachers should also show respect to their students.

3 Some people feel that there has been an increase in crimes, but the police say that crimes have not increased.

4 My sister bought a nice bookmark for me in New York City. Unfortunately, I can't bookmark web pages with it. ☺

14 Word families

Use the word given in capitals at the end of each line to form another word of the same word family that fits in the sentence in the same line.

1 "Please print ______ out the form and sign it." – "I'm sorry, but my ______ is broken."	PRINT
2 Tom helped his parents with the ______ of his sister's birthday party.	ORGANIZE
3 It's easy to go to Berlin by train. There are excellent ______ between most German towns and cities.	CONNECT
4 Jim's family is very poor because his parents have been ______ for a long time now.	EMPLOY
5 ______ can make people ill.	POOR
6 Are these streets ______ at night?	SAFETY
7 Finding a cheap flat is a big ______ in cities all over the world these days.	CHALLENGE

15 Synonyms

Read the sentences and find a word that has the same meaning as the underlined word in each sentence.

1 Oh, that's a really bad cut! ______

2 That's a long story – where do I start? ______

3 Wild animals, for example, rabbits and deer, died in the fires. ______

16 New words SB pp. 38–41

Write the missing words in the crossword.

1 when groups of people walk, hold signs, and sing or shout to express their opinion about something
2 What a ??? that you can't come to my party!
3 ►► (to) join (a group activity) *(Find two words.)*
4 (to) live through a very dangerous or very difficult situation
5 (to) pull something into smaller pieces, usually with violence
6 four letters that stand for different forms of sexuality or gender identity
7 (to) make someone or something part of a group
8 ◄► noise
9 ►► holy
10 someone who works in or wants to work in the government
11 being straight, lesbian or gay are all forms of people's ???
12 a group of people who have agreed to support each other
13 (to) cut hair off your face or other parts of your body
14 the leader of a Native American tribe

15 ►► a long talk that somebody gives to a person or group of people
16 ◄► gay/lesbian
17 Your ??? is on the outside of your body.
18 all activities connected to the believing in a god or gods
19 (to) say or show that you disagree with sth.
20 knowing sth. because you have seen or done it

My learner log

★ My three favourite words in this unit are:

____

I can …

- talk about Native Americans *(Write six words that are connected to Native Americans.)*:

  ____

  ____

- discuss gun laws in the USA *(Write two sentences with your opinion about gun laws in the USA.)*:

  ____

  ____

What was difficult in Unit 2:

____

What was easy in Unit 2:

____

What I liked about Unit 2:

____

1 Revision: Units 1 & 2

1 Volumes and …

a) There are six words in the word search (↑ ↓ → ←). Find and circle them. Then read the sentences and complete them with these words.

b) The letters in the dark fields form an umbrella word for the six words. Put them in the correct order and write the word: ______________________

D	E	G	R	E	E
U	R	A	T	R	R
M	T	L	S	E	T
M	I	L	E	M	E
E	L	O	A	S	M
H	C	N	I	E	N

1 An ______________ is 2.54 cm.

2 100 cm is one ______________.

3 A ______________ is about 1.6 km.

4 Water boils at 100 ______________s Celsius.

5 An American ______________ is less than a British one.

6 In Germany we measure water, milk or petrol in ______________s.

2 Word families

Use the word given in capitals at the end of each line to form another word of the same word family that fits in the sentence in the same line.

1 There are some ______________ differences between Germany and the USA.	**CULTURE**
2 Finishing school is a big ______________ for students.	**ACHIEVE**
3 When you travel to the USA you have to fill in an ______________ form.	**APPLY**
4 Emma Gonzáles gave a ______________ in Fort Lauderdale.	**SPEAK**
5 Emma was one of the ______________ of the mass shooting at her school.	**SURVIVAL**

3 What are they doing?

Write what the people in the pictures are doing. Use the present progressive.

1 Jess is on her way to New York. Here she is ____________ ____ at the airport.

2 After the flight she needs a coffee. Here she's buying one from a ____________ ____________.

3 Now Jess is ____________ a meeting at her company.

4 Matt is ____________ the internet for information on a protest march in his town.

5 Matt is ____________ the information he found on the internet.

6 Now Matt and his friends are ____________ ________ in the protest march.

4 What has happened to them?

Write what has happened to the people in the pictures. Use the present perfect.

1 Their car ____________ ________. They need to phone for help.

2 Jim ____________ his driving test. Now he is allowed to drive a car on his own.

3 Molly ____________ her new dress. She's very unhappy.

5 Opposites

Write the opposites.

1 correct ◄► ____________

2 awake ◄► ____________

3 dangerous ◄► ____________

4 fake ◄► ____________

5 noise ◄► ____________

6 less ◄► ____________

Unit 3 A changing world

1 New words SB pp. 44–45

What do the following words mean? Match the expressions (A–E) with their corresponding definitions (1–7). Write the correct numbers in the grid below. Be careful: There are two definitions that you do not need.

A (to) improve
B product
C volunteer
D assembly line
E robot

1 the area in a factory where parts of a product are put together, piece by piece
2 someone who works for free, often for a charity
3 a machine that is designed to do specific tasks, often very quickly
4 (to) act in a play
5 something that people buy or use for free
6 a group of students waiting for the teacher
7 (to) become better or make something better

A	B	C	D	E

2 New words SB p. 46

Look at the picture and write the English words.

1 ______
2 ______
3 ______
4 ______
5 ______

3 More car words

Write the missing words in the gaps.

Every car needs an **1** e______ to move. Most cars have four **2** w______. Cars usually have three **3** m______ so that the driver can see the traffic behind him or her. If you want to drive a car, you need a **4** d______ l______.

4 New words SB pp. 46–47

a) Write the English words under the pictures.

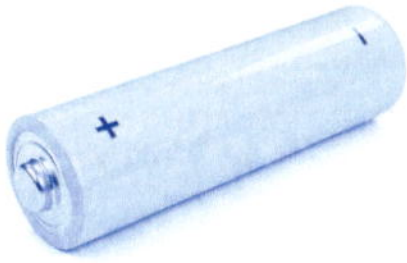

1 ______________ 2 ______________ 3 ______________ 4 ______________

b) What do the following words mean? Match the expressions (A–I) with their corresponding definitions (1–10). Write the correct numbers in the grid below. Be careful: There is one definition that you do not need.

A appliance
B data
C disability
D goods
E network
F privacy
G (to) repair
H security
I space

1 something that makes it more difficult to do specific things
2 a group of things, such as computers, that are connected to each other
3 the state of being alone and not watched by anyone
4 (to) make something that is broken work again
5 the state of being safe
6 a machine that does specific jobs in the home
7 ►► room
8 not showing respect
9 facts or information
10 things that you can buy or sell

A	B	C	D	E	F	G	H	I

c) Read the sentences and complete them with the words from the box. Use the correct form of the words.

complex • in addition • may • (to) prevent • (to) program • (to) reduce (by) • (to) solve • (to) track • (to) transport • (to) unlock

1 Will self-driving cars really ______________________ accidents?

2 Computer programs are very ______________________ and often difficult to understand.

3 Sarah wants to learn Spanish. She ______________________ even go to Spain for a few months.

4 John lost his key, so he can't ______________________ his bike now.

5 Driving too fast is dangerous. ______________________, it's bad for the environment.

6 Students should learn to ______________________ computers.

7 Lorries can ______________________ heavy goods.

8 If they ______________________ the price of fares, more people will use public transport.

9 Sam has tried to ______________________ the maths exercise for hours.

10 Websites ______________________ people who visit them and collect their data.

5 New words SB *p. 48*

Write the English words in the gaps.

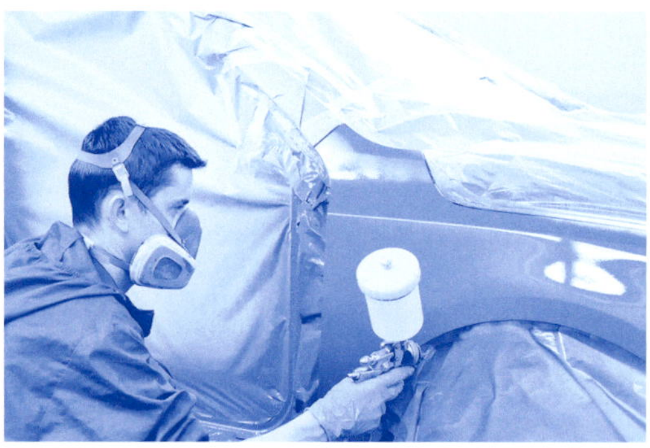

Kim is **1** ______________________ *(lackieren)* the **2** ______________________ *(Karosserie)* of a car.

Sam is **3** ______________________ *(schweißen)* parts of a car together.

6 New words SB p. 49

Write the missing words in the crossword.

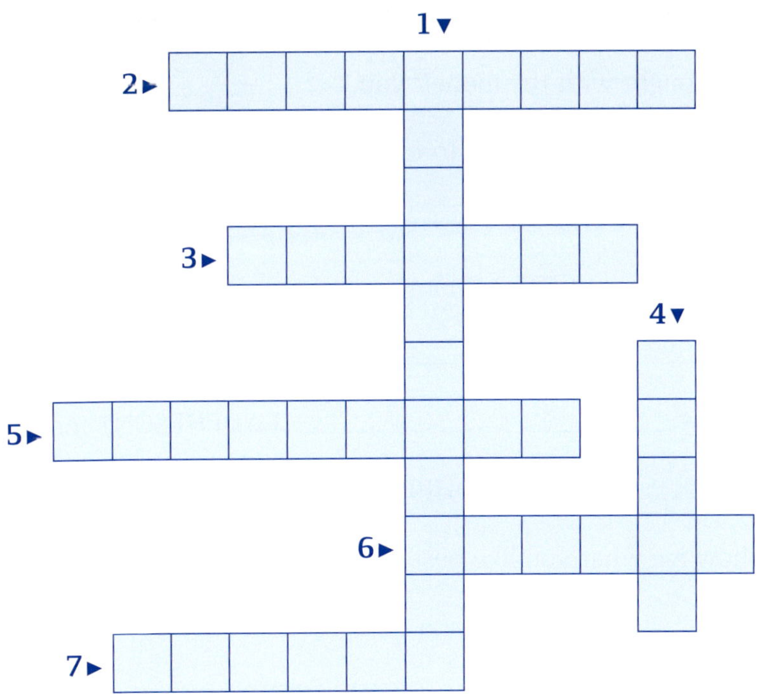

1 it makes machines or lamps work; even cars can run on it, if they don't run on petrol

2 all the people living together in a house or flat

3 the way you do or make something, especially in industry

4 1,000 kg

5 when materials are put into the environment that harm it or make it dirty

6 (to) create or think something for the first time

7 what oil, water, the sun or the wind give us

7 How to say it

Where is the stress in the words in ***bold****? Circle the part of the word that you stress when you say it.*

1 Can you please leave the room? I'd like some **privacy**.

2 It took us hours to **program** the new machines.

3 This sounds like a **complex** problem.

4 We must **prevent** fires to save wild animals.

5 Car sharing is a popular form of **transport**.

6 Jim has a learning **disability**.

7 We should use more clean **energy**.

8 New words SB p. 50

Complete the sentences with the scrambled words[1] in brackets.

Lucy: This is the **1** ____________________ (RUALTIV) reality headset that I bought with the money you gave me for my birthday! Would you like to try it?

Grandma: Yes, please. Don't we have to plug the **2** ____________________ (STSYME) into my phone or your PC to make it work?

Lucy: No, we don't. It's a **3** ____________________ (NDAST-LAONE) headset. It came complete with **4** ____________________ (EADPHESON) and a **5** ____________________ (ONECROHPIM).

Grandma: How interesting. Show me what you like best about it.

Lucy: It has lots of great **6** ____________________ (UREATFES), for example, it's very light, and the **7** ____________________ (HGRASCIP) are very **8** ____________________ (STICLIREA), as you can see in this 3D game.

Grandma: Oh, yes, I can see that. It's fantastic.

9 New words SB p. 51

Read the sentences and complete them with the words from the box. Use the correct form of the words.

announcement • at least • once • radio • (to) recognize • (to) record • radio station • success

Dear Hector,

I often listen to the **1** ____________________ and I always **2** ____________________ your voice when you make an **3** ____________________ .

Do you think it is possible to volunteer at your **4** ____________________ **5** ____________________ a week? I have **6** ____________________ my voice and included the mp3 file in this email. I know the road to **7** ____________________ is difficult – but **8** ____________________ I have made a start now. ☺

Best wishes, Luke

[1] scrambled word *Schüttelwort*

GO »
AHEAD
REALSCHULE BAYERN

Wordmaster

8

Lösungen

The USA: facts and figures

1 New words SB pp. 8–9

1 km², square kilometres **2** melting pot **3** cultural **4** broke away **5** stripes **6** everyday **7** impression **8** Midwest **9** measurements **10** miles **11** volume **12** litres **13** gallons **14** degrees **15** Fahrenheit

1 The American dream

1 New words SB pp. 10–11

1 check in **2** Liberty **3** masses **4** huddled **5** definition **6** personal **7** African American **8** ancestors **9** yearned for **10** yearned to **11** achieved **12** perform

2 New words SB pp. 12–13

1 interpret **2** lyrics **3** boroughs **4** route **5** subway **6** freedom **7** state of mind **8** financial

3 New words SB pp. 14–15

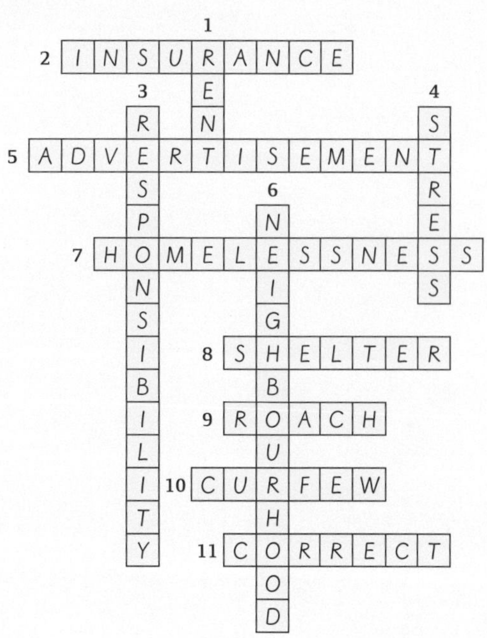

4 Word families

1 Freedom **2** check-in **3** Homelessness **4** mass **5** performance **6** personal

5 Verbs and nouns and what they mean in German

a) **1** ((to) rent) – mieten, leihen – rent – Miete
2 (to) advertise – Werbung machen für etw. – (advertisement) – Anzeige, Inserat; Werbespot
3 (to) stress – betonen – stress – (Betonung)
4 (to) achieve – erreichen, erzielen, schaffen – achievement – (Errungenschaft, Leistung)

b) **1** advertise **2** stress **3** achievement **4** rent

6 New words SB p. 16

1 applicants **2** enter **3** citizenship **4** property **5** issue **6** expiration **7** apply for **8** addict **9** committed **10** harm

7 New words SB p. 17

1 booked **2** first floor **3** traffic **4** closets **5** change **6** fare **7** vending machine **8** coffee **9** receptionist **10** key card **11** waiters and waitresses **12** tip **13** bill

8 American English – British English

1 subway – (underground) – U-Bahn
2 (neighborhood) – neighbourhood – Nachbarschaft, Gegend, Viertel
3 first floor – ground floor – Erdgeschoss
4 third floor – (second floor) – zweiter Stock
5 (second floor) – first floor – erster Stock
6 (expiration) – expiry – Ablauf, Verfall

7 closet – (wardrobe/cupboard) – (Wand-)Schrank

9 New words SB pp. 18–21

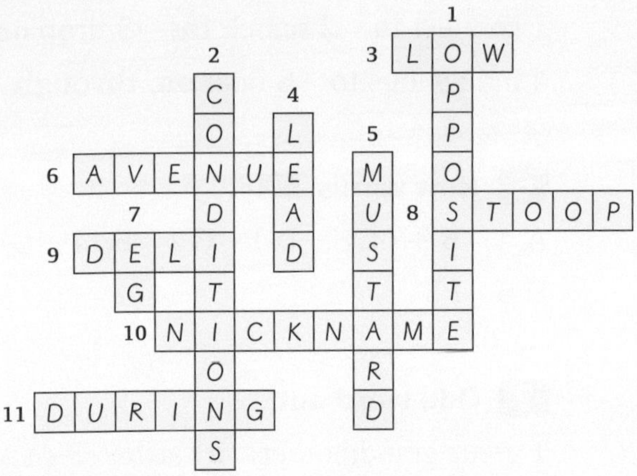

10 How to say it

1 ancestors 2 definition 3 financial
4 interpret 5 curfew 6 insurance
7 volume

11 New words SB p. 22

a) 1 sneaker *(AE)*, trainer *(BE)*
2 overweight 3 skinny 4 makeup
5 cheek 6 mosquito

b) 1 vibrated 2 as soon as
3 professional 4 acted 5 résumé; promise; schedule 6 manicure

c) 1 E 2 G 3 C 4 F 5 B 6 A 7 D

12 New words SB p. 23

a) 1 a once-over 2 tight
3 take my eyes off 4 appreciate
5 sweating 6 heels 7 inches

b) 1 entrance 2 store/shop 3 counter
4 guard 5 restroom *(AE)*, toilet *(BE)*
6 helicopter 7 (light) bulb
8 cell (phone) *(AE)*, mobile (phone) *(BE)*

13 New words SB p. 25

A	B	C	D	E	F	G
4	7	6	5	2	1	3

14 American English – British English

1 cell phone – (mobile (phone)) – Handy
2 store – (shop) – Geschäft
3 (restroom) – toilet – Toilette
4 (sidewalk) – pavement – Bürgersteig
5 vacation – (holiday) – Urlaub, Ferien
6 gas station – (petrol station) – Tankstelle
7 (sneaker) – trainer – Sportschuh
8 mom – (mum) – Mama, Mutti

15 Opposites

1 (to) check out 2 low 3 skinny 4 poor
5 strong 6 short

16 Crossword

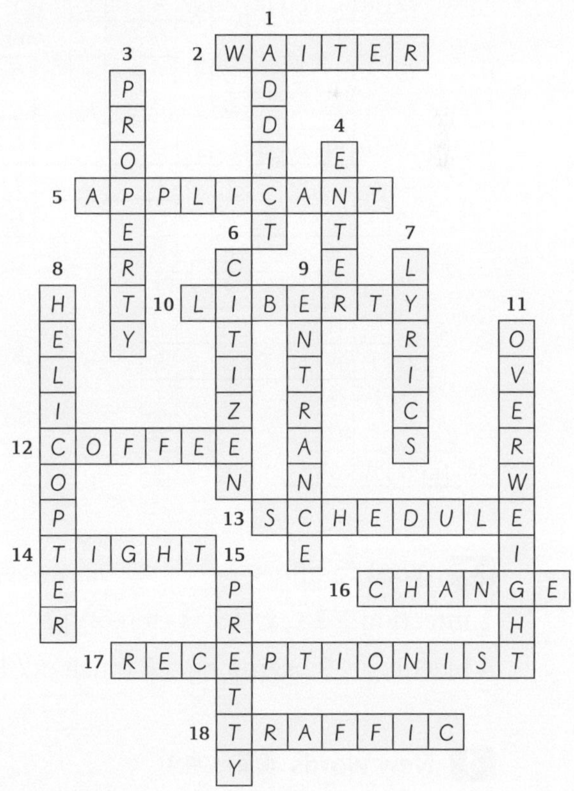

17 Synonyms

1 mobile 2 store 3 liberty 4 great
5 correct

2 Land of the free?

1 New words SB pp. 26–27

1 reservation **2** (to) search (for sth.) **3** aspect **4** braid **5** exhibition **6** tribal elder **7** adobe **8** bead **9** jewellery **10** feathers **11** native **12** indigenous (to) **13** headdress **14** stereotype **15** Native Americans **16** member

2 New words SB pp. 28–29

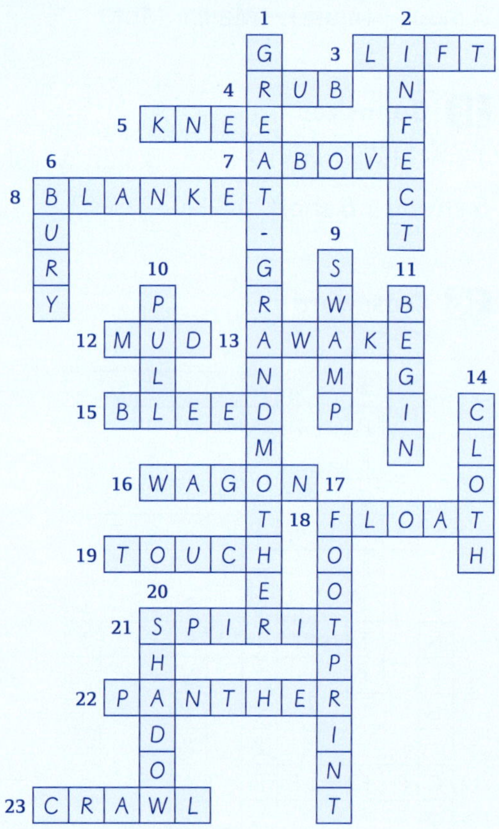

3 Word families

1 infection **2** search **3** stereotypes **4** bleeding **5** beginning **6** touch **7** lift

4 New words SB pp. 30–31

1 poverty **2** gun **3** drunk driving **4** alcohol **5** driving licence *(BE)*/driver's license *(AE)* **6** unemployed **7** challenge **8** dropped out **9** connect **10** difficult **11** minimum

5 Prepositions

1 connect **to** **2** search **for** **3** drop **out** **4** indigenous **to** **5** float **on**, **through**

6 New words SB p. 32

A 4 **B** 9 **C** 8 **D** 1 **E** 2 **F** 11 **G** 5 **H** 6 **I** 3

7 Odd word out

1 great-grandmother **2** cattle **3** camera **4** expiry **5** poverty

8 Opposites

1 below **2** difficult/hard **3** maximum **4** (to) begin/(to) start

9 New words SB p. 33

1 Camerawork **2** inspiring **3** poor **4** grandson/granddaughter **5** grandson/granddaughter **6** campfire **7** breaks down **8** fantastic **9** nasty **10** wise **11** respectful

10 New words SB pp. 34–35

1 debate **2** chairperson **3** law **4** safety **5** guy **6** suicides **7** increased **8** control **9** thanked

11 New words SB p. 36

A 5 **B** 7 **C** 8 **D** 9 **E** 10 **F** 12 **G** 11 **H** 2 **I** 1 **J** 4 **K** 6 **L** 3

12 New words SB p. 37

1 such a **2** passed **3** such as **4** automatic

13 Verbs and nouns

1 My parents and their friends often debate about important things, but I didn't understand what last night's debate was about.

2 Students should respect their teachers, but teachers should also show respect to their students.

3 Some people feel that there has been an increase in crimes, but the police say that crimes have not increased.

4 My sister bought a nice bookmark for me in New York City. Unfortunately, I can't bookmark web pages with it. ☺

14 Word families

1 print; printer **2** organization
3 connections **4** unemployed
5 Poverty **6** safe **7** challenge

15 Synonyms

1 nasty **2** begin **3** such as

16 New words SB pp. 38–41

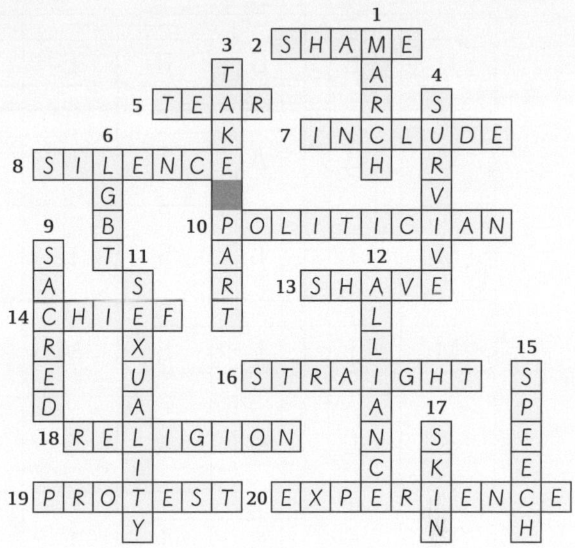

Revision 1&2

1 Volumes and …

measurements

D	E	G	R	E	E
U	R	A	T	R	R
M	T	L	S	E	T
M	I	L	E	M	E
E	L	O	A	S	M
H	C	N	I	E	N

1 inch **2** metre **3** mile **4** degrees
5 gallon **6** litres

2 Word families

1 cultural **2** achievement **3** application
4 speech **5** survivors

3 What are they doing?

1 checking in **2** vending machine
3 leading **4** searching **5** print (out)
6 taking part

4 What has happened to them?

1 has broken down **2** has passed
3 has torn

5 Opposites

1 wrong/incorrect **2** asleep **3** safe
4 real/true **5** silence **6** more

3 A changing world

1 New words SB *pp. 44–45*

A 7 **B** 5 **C** 2 **D** 1 **E** 3

2 New words SB *p. 46*

1 roof **2** seat **3** steering wheel
4 tyre **5** windscreen

3 More car words

1 engine **2** wheels **3** mirrors
4 driving licence *(BE)*/driver's license *(AE)*

4 New words SB *pp. 46–47*

a) **1** pillow **2** drone **3** speaker
4 battery

b) **A** 6 **B** 9 **C** 1 **D** 10 **E** 2 **F** 3
G 4 **H** 5 **I** 7

c) **1** prevent **2** complex **3** may
4 unlock **5** In addition **6** program
7 transport **8** reduce **9** solve **10** track

5 New words SB *p. 48*

1 painting **2** body **3** welding

6 New words SB *p. 49*

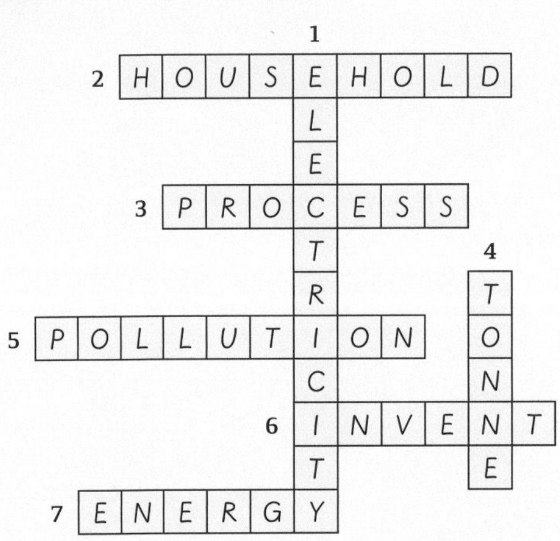

7 How to say it

1 privacy **2** program **3** complex
4 prevent **5** transport **6** disability
7 energy

8 New words SB *p. 50*

1 virtual **2** system **3** stand-alone
4 headphones **5** microphone **6** features
7 graphics **8** realistic

9 New words SB *p. 51*

1 radio **2** recognize **3** announcement
4 radio station **5** once **6** recorded
7 success **8** at least

10 New words SB *pp. 52–53*

1 sculpture **2** installation **3** stuff
4 toys **5** sustainable **6** Instead of
7 reuse **8** details **9** reminds **10** cause
11 yard **12** replace **13** colourful
14 necessary

11 New words SB *p. 54*

1 chemicals **2** Therefore **3** made
4 organic **5** properly **6** zippers
7 grow **8** Since **9** pockets **10** last
11 overall **12** value

12 Word families

1 improvement **2** disability **3** private
4 invention **5** successful

13 New words SB *p. 55*

a) **A** 4 **B** 1 **C** 2

b) **1** full stop **2** question mark
3 exclamation mark **4** comma
5 colon **6** hyphen

14 New words SB p. 56

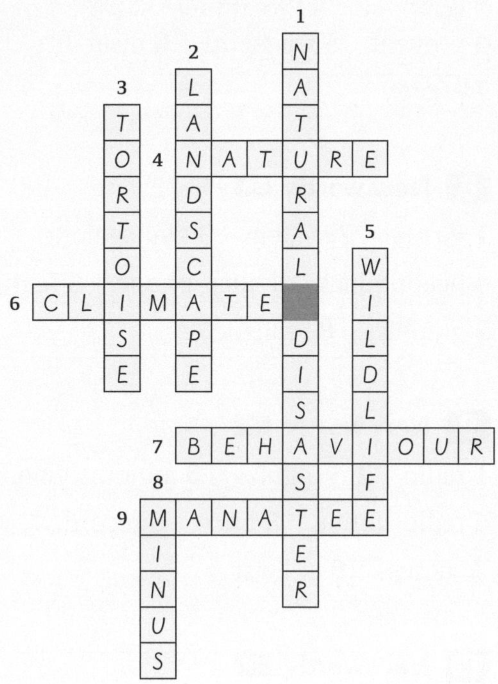

15 New words SB pp. 57–59

a) **A** 7 **B** 6 **C** 8 **D** 2 **E** 3 **F** 5 **G** 4 **H** 1

b) **1** draws **2** Climbing **3** peaceful **4** play dead **5** threatened **6** rose **7** speed

16 Odd word out

1 volunteer **2** nature **3** cat

17 Verbs and nouns

1 You can repair this camera, that kind of repair is always very expensive.

2 You need a strong lock for your bike if you want to lock it in front of your house.

3 Nobody knows exactly what causes accidents on motorways, but one of the causes is drivers checking their mobile phones.

4 Last month Jane's house was flooded for the third time this year, but the floods before weren't as bad as this one.

5 Lots of people think we're on the wrong track if we allow website owners to track our data.

4 Black lives

1 New words SB pp. 60–61

a) **1** slavery **2** passed a law **3** Civil War **4** civil rights **5** segregation **6** education **7** activists **8** discrimination

b) **1** wife **2** (to) be afraid (of) **3** lawyer **4** hurricane **5** (to) mediate **6** role model **7** Mardi Gras **8** mostly

2 New words SB p. 62

1 neighbourhood watch **2** suspicious **3** victim **4** armed **5** bullets **6** chase **7** go on with **8** matters **9** lie **10** charged **11** murder **12** court **13** trial **14** cleared of **15** prison

3 New words SB p. 63

A 8 **B** 12 **C** 1 **D** 2 **E** 9 **F** 3 **G** 11 **H** 5 **I** 6 **J** 4

4 Not many

1 a few **2** few **3** little **4** a little **5** a few **6** few

5 New words SB pp. 64–67

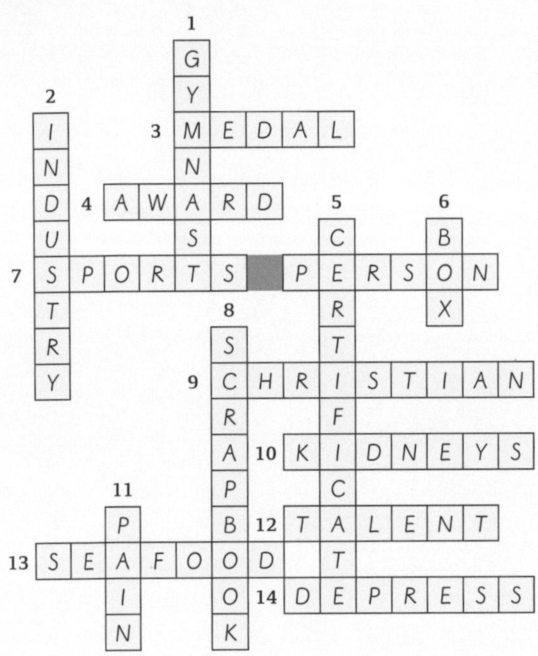

6 New words SB pp. 68–70

1 shocking **2** destroyed **3** condition **4** rebuilt **5** tornado **6** mayor **7** level **8** power **9** disgusted **10** grew up **11** graduated **12** Anyway

7 Word families

1 awareness **2** racial **3** education **4** murderer **5** charged **6** Slavery

8 New words SB p. 71

1 appointment **2** temperature **3** pills **4** antibiotic **5** prescription **6** documents **7** allergy **8** drugstore **9** twice

9 Phrases with (to) take

1 temperature **2** seat **3** taking photos/pictures **4** taking notes **5** taking (a) rest/break **6** taking (a) test **7** taking (his) blood pressure **8** taking part

10 New words SB p. 72

a) **1** bee **2** flashlight *(AE)*, torch *(BE)* **3** wallet **4** ticket **5** badge **6** scar **7** dashboard **8** buzz cut

b) **A** 11 **B** 8 **C** 5 **D** 2 **E** 3 **F** 9 **G** 4 **H** 10 **I** 7 **J** 1 **K** 6

11 American English – British English

1 baggage – (luggage) – Gepäck
2 (candy) – sweets – Süßigkeiten
3 grade – ((school) year) – Schuljahr
4 cookie – biscuit – Keks
5 (driver's license) – driving licence – Führerschein, Fahrerlaubnis
6 elevator – (lift) – Fahrstuhl, Lift
7 movie theater – (cinema) – Kino
8 schedule – (timetable) – Zeitplan, Stundenplan

12 New words SB pp. 73–75

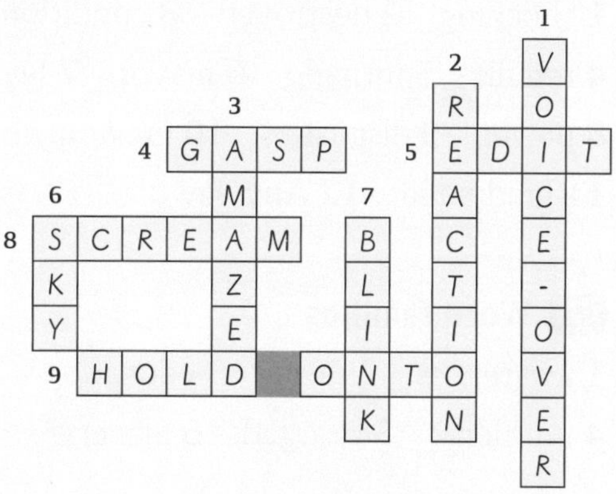

13 Verbs and nouns – same spelling, different pronunciation

1 increase **2** protest **3** record

4 transport

14 Verbs and nouns

1 We usually access our drive from the main road, but at the moment access for cars is not allowed.

2 Lots of people rent their flat or house, but for some it has become difficult to pay the rent.

3 Sue and Dave have been volunteers at the zoo for many years, but this year Sue also volunteers in a children's home.

4 Jim plays in a band and often records their practice. He also collects records.

5 Lots of young people protest against climate change and join protest marches.

Revision 3&4

1 Definitions

A 7 **B** 10 **C** 8 **D** 1 **E** 2 **F** 3

G 5 **H** 6 **I** 4 **J** 9

2 What are the people doing?

1 repairing **2** (un)locking **3** climbing

4 drawing

3 Crossword – American English and British English

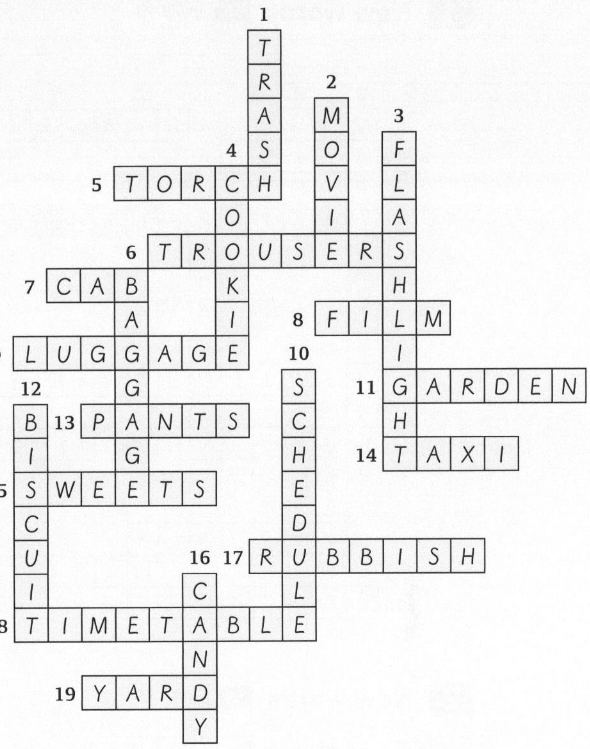

5 In Canada

1 New words SB pp. 78–79

2 New words SB p. 80

1 alert **2** frightening **3** horns **4** flashing
5 weighs **6** kilos **7** fear **8** migration
9 Bay **10** traps **11** seal **12** sense

3 New words SB pp. 81

1 scalp **2** attitude **3** terrified **4** shovel
5 autumn **6** local **7** grabbed

4 Adjectives

1 boring **2** embarrassing **3** amazing
4 disappointed **5** exciting **6** surprised
7 worried **8** depressing

5 Word families

1 happiness **2** emphasize/emphasise *(BE)*
3 aware **4** bilingual **5** Migration/Migrating
6 weight

6 New words SB pp. 82–83

1 outdoors **2** adventures **3** canoeing
4 fishing **5** suggestions **6** make excuses
7 confirm

7 New words SB pp. 84–85

A 7 **B** 5 **C** 6 **D** 8 **E** 4 **F** 3 **G** 1 **H** 2

8 Word families

1 education **2** reduce **3** invention
4 treatment **5** Pollution **6** weakness

9 New words SB pp. 86–87

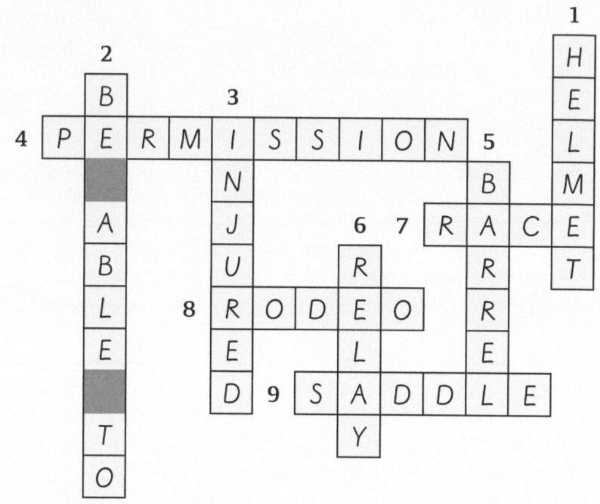

10 How to say it

1 diagrams **2** polar **3** mosaic
4 legend **5** rodeos

11 New words SB p. 88

1 Dear Sir or Madam **2** cruelty **3** straps
4 buck **5** possible **6** Finally
7 publish **8** Yours faithfully

12 New words SB p. 89

1 bar chart **2** info graphic **3** line chart
4 five in a **5** development

13 New words SB p. 90

a) **A** 11 **B** 9 **C** 10 **D** 1 **E** 4 **F** 2
G 7 **H** 12 **I** 6 **J** 5 **K** 3 **L** 8

b) **1** cabin **2** jar **3** hatchet **4** shore
5 whistle **6** edge **7** branch **8** tail

14 New words SB pp. 91–93

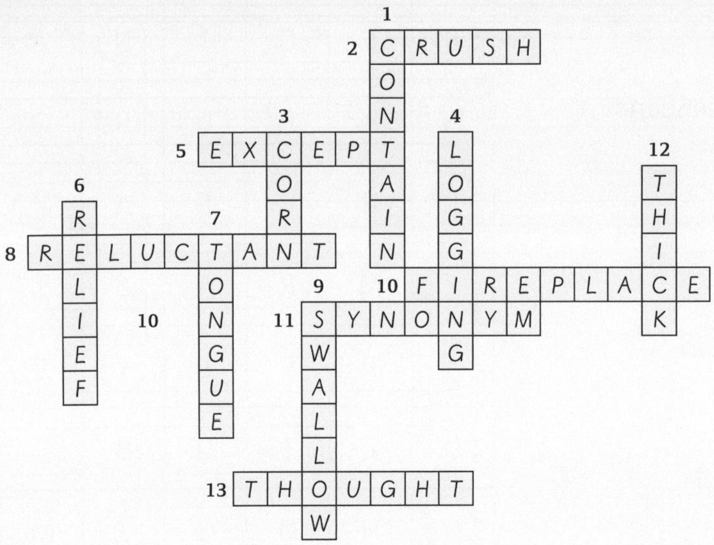

15 The fourth word

1 autumn **2** shovel **3** mouth **4** tail
5 branch **6** saddle

16 Prepositions

1 applied **for**, **at** the local hospital
2 belongs **to** **3** connected **to**
4 graduate **from** **5** increased **by**
6 Point **to** **7** refers **to**
8 searched **for** **9** take part **in**
10 staring **at** **11** yearns **for** **12** reach **for**
13 **in** 100 ten-year-olds

17 Opposites

1 descendant **2** thin **3** apart
4 neither … nor **5** at the end/finally

Finale

1 Compounds

assembly line – Montageband, Fließband
buzz cut – Igelfrisur
cell phone *(AE)* – Handy
civil rights – Bürgerrechte
civil war – Bürgerkrieg
driver's license *(AE)* – Führerschein
global warming – Erderwärmung
health care – Gesundheitsfürsorge, medizinische Versorgung
maple leaf – Ahornblatt
melting pot – Schmelztiegel
natural disaster – Naturkatastrophe
neighbourhood watch – Nachbarschaftswache
polar bear – Eisbär
tribal elder – Stammesälteste/r

2 Useful objects and what you use them for

(Mögliche Lösungen)

2 Drones can transport light goods in the air. You can also take photos from above with them.
3 I use headphones to listen to music, etc.
4 I sleep in a sleeping bag when I go camping.
5 I dig a hole with a shovel.
6 I put money and cards in my wallet.

3 Who are they?

A 4 **B** 5 **C** 10 **D** 7 **E** 8 **F** 9 **G** 3
H 6 **I** 1 **J** 2

4 Verbs

B	E	G	I	N	A	Q
W	A	R	D	R	O	P
L	B	R	E	A	K	J
E	M	R	A	E	T	W
A	P	P	L	Y	R	O
D	L	I	U	B	E	R
S	H	O	O	T	M	G

1 was shot **2** drawing **3** began
4 drop; break **5** has applied **6** tore
7 grew **8** lead **9** is yearning **10** rebuilt

5 Crossword

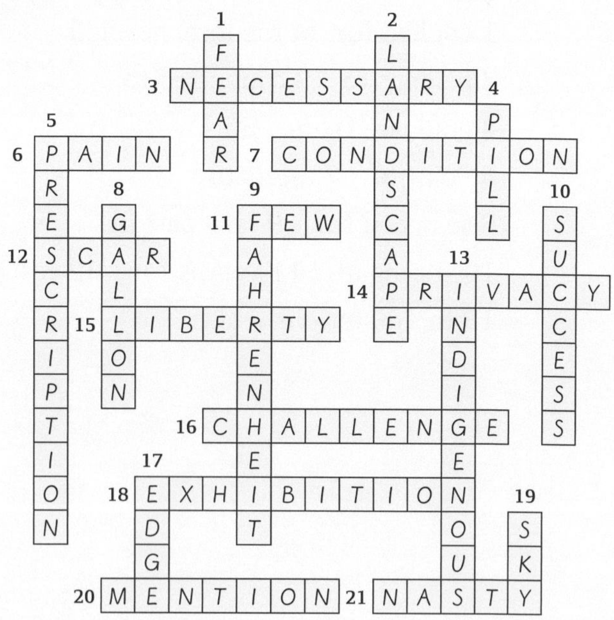

10 New words SB pp. 52–53

Read the sentences and complete them with the words from the box. Use the correct form of the words.

(to) cause • colourful • detail • installation • instead of • necessary • (to) remind • (to) replace • (to) reuse • sculpture • stuff • sustainable • toy • yard

What a great **1** ________________!

What kind of art

2 ________________

is this? Look, it's old

3 ________________ and

children's **4** ________________.

That's a **5** ________________

form of art. **6** ________________

throwing old things away you

7 ________________ them.

Look, it has some nice

8 ________________ too.

Actually, it **9** ________________

me of something I made at

school.

Do you think it would

10 ________________ much

trouble to make something like that

for our **11** ________________?

We could

12 ________________

that dead tree with something more

13 ________________.

It's **14** ________________ to

cut down that tree anyway.

11 New words SB p. 54

Read the adverts and complete them with the words from the box.

chemicals • grow • last • made • organic • overall • pockets • properly • since • therefore • value • zippers

We don't like selling clothes that are full of **1** ______________ and break after you buy them. **2** ______________ all our clothes are **3** ______________ of **4** ______________ materials, and they're made **5** ______________. Only the **6** ______________ are metal and metal doesn't **7** ______________ on trees!

8 ______________ people need room for all kinds of stuff these days, our jeans come with extra large **9** ______________. Buy them and never worry about where to put your phone or your car keys again.

You want home appliances that will **10** ______________ for a long time? – We offer appliances with an excellent **11** ______________ quality and good **12** ______________ for money. Check our company website for details.

12 Word families

Use the word given in capitals at the end of each line to form another word of the same word family that fits in the sentence in the same line.

1 Mr Cox saw a big ______________ in David's work.	IMPROVE
2 John's ______________ doesn't stop him from doing sports.	DISABLED
3 The hotel is fantastic. Each room has a ______________ bathroom.	PRIVACY
4 The wheel was a very important ______________.	INVENT
5 The party was very ______________. People enjoyed themselves.	SUCCESS

13 New words SB p. 55

a) Match the words with the explanations. There is one definition that you don't need.

A content

B grammar

C punctuation

1 the rules in a language according to which you put words into their correct forms and build sentences

2 signs that you use when you are writing a text to help the reader understand what you mean

3 the way that things are joined together

4 what is inside something

b) Write the English words next to the pictures.

1  ______________

2  ______________ ______________

3  ______________ ______________

4  ______________

5  ______________

6  ______________

14 New words SB p. 56

Write the missing words in the crossword.

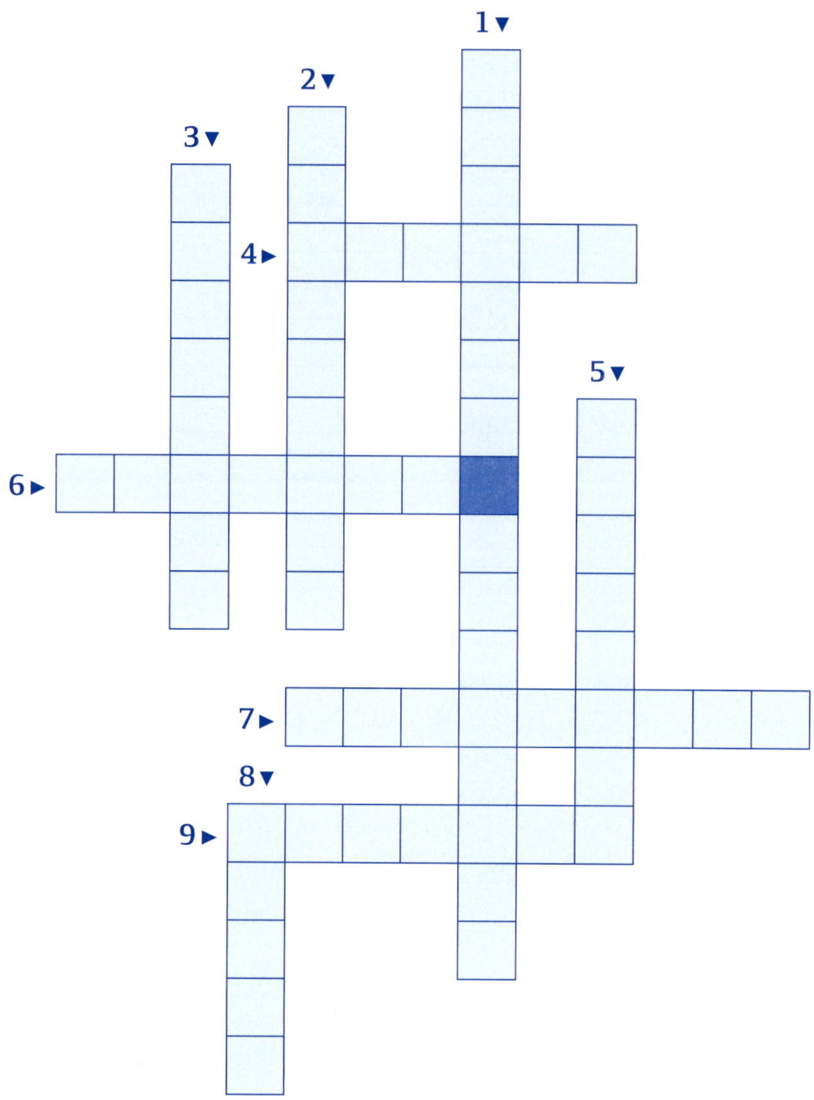

1 Terrible events such as earthquakes, storms or big fires can be a ???. *(Find two words.)*

2 everything you can see when you look across an area

3 

4 all things, animals and plants in the world that aren't made by people

5 all animals and plants that live in a natural environment

6 the weather conditions of a place, over a long time

7 the way that you do things or act around people

8 ◄► plus

9 

15 New words SB pp. 57–59

a) What do the following words mean? Match the expressions (A–H) with their corresponding definitions (1–8). Write the correct numbers in the grid below.

A thin
B drought
C global warming
D wildfire
E flood
F diet
G salmon
H sleeping bag

1 a big warm blanket with a zipper that you use at night when you go camping
2 when grass and trees in a large area are burning
3 a lot of water in an area that is usually dry
4 a large fish that is pink inside and often used for food
5 the food that you usually eat
6 a long time without rain
7 ◄► fat
8 the fact that temperatures have risen all over the world

A	B	C	D	E	F	G	H

b) Read the sentences and complete them with the words from the box. Use the correct form of the words.

(to) climb • (to) draw • peaceful • (to) play dead • (to) rise • speed • (to) threaten

1 Alicia is very good at art. She ______________ beautiful pictures.

2 ______________ is a very popular sport.

3 John lives in a small and ______________ village in the mountains.

4 People say that you should ______________ if a brown bear attacks you.

5 Wild animals are ______________ by fires, floods and droughts.

6 It didn't stop raining, and some rivers ______________ dangerously.

7 Drivers must reduce ______________ near schools and hospitals.

16 Odd word out

Circle the odd word out.

1 robot – appliance – drone – volunteer

2 colourful – sustainable – nature – organic

3 manatee – cat – salmon – whale

17 Verbs and nouns

Read the sentences. Some verbs and nouns are in the same form. Circle these nouns and underline these verbs.

1 You can repair this camera, but that kind of repair is always very expensive.

2 You need a strong lock for your bike if you want to lock it in front of your house.

3 Nobody knows exactly what causes accidents on motorways, but one of the causes is drivers checking their mobile phones.

4 Last month Jane's house was flooded for the third time this year, but the floods before weren't as bad as this one.

5 Lots of people think we're on the wrong track if we allow website owners to track our data.

My learner log

★ My three favourite words in this unit are:

____

I can …

- describe (smart) technology *(Write six words from the world of technology.)*:

____

____

- talk about natural parks *(Write one sentence to describe a national park. Write one sentence about the dangers national parks are faced with.)*:

____

____

What was difficult in Unit 3:

____

What was easy in Unit 3:

____

What I liked about Unit 3:

____

Black lives

Unit 4

1 New words SB pp. 60–61

a) Read the sentences and complete them with the words from the box.

activists • civil rights • Civil War • discrimination • education • passed a law • segregation • slavery

The history of many African Americans begins with **1** ______________ in the 17th and 18th century: Lots of their ancestors were brought to America and had to work as slaves. At the beginning of the 19th century the United States **2** ______________ against the slave trade, but slave trade didn't stop. In the mid-19th century the U. S. became divided between slave states in the south and free states in the north, and in 1861 the **3** ______________ started between the North and the South. In 1865 all slaves were free and were given **4** ______________. But a few years later some southern states took away these rights, and many years of **5** ______________ followed: Black people couldn't use the same restaurants or restrooms as white people. Black and white children couldn't get an **6** ______________ at the same school. Lots of **7** ______________ fought against this, and in 1964 the Civil Rights Act banned all **8** ______________ by law.

b) Read the definitions and write the words from the box next to them.

(to) be afraid (of) • (to) mediate • hurricane • lawyer • Mardi Gras • mostly • role model • wife

1 a woman who is married: ______________

2 ►► (to) be scared (of): ______________

3 someone who gives people advice about the law: ______________

4 a dangerous storm: ______________

5 (to) help people who are fighting to find a solution: ______________

6 a person whose behaviour other people try to copy: ______________

7 the name of the carnival in New Orleans: ______________

8 ►► usually, mainly: ______________

2 New words SB p. 62

Complete the dialogue with the words from the box.

armed • bullets • charged with • chase • cleared of • court • go on • lie • matters • murder • neighbourhood watch • prison • suspicious • trial • victim

George: My father is in a **1** ______________ ______________ group. These people try to prevent crime in our area, and report unusual or **2** ______________ activity to the police.

Kyra: Isn't your dad scared to become a **3** ______________ himself? The person he follows might be **4** ______________ *(bewaffnet)*. What if someone has a gun, and there are **5** ______________ in it?

George: Dad and the other members of the group are very careful. They don't **6** ______________ *(verfolgen)* people. Mom worries too sometimes, but I think Dad will **7** ______________ doing it because he thinks that what he does for our area really **8** ______________. He's not the kind of person to **9** ______________ around and watch TV.

Kyra: Has your dad ever reported a really dangerous activity to the police?

George: Yes, once he reported someone who was **10** ______________ *(angeklagt mit)* **11** ______________ *(Mord)*. The person had been hiding in our garden! There was a report from **12** ______________ every day on TV about the **13** ______________ against that person. The man hoped to be **14** ______________ the charges, but he was sent to **15** ______________ for life.

Kyra: Wow, your dad really does a great job!

3 New words SB p.63

What do the following words mean? Match the expressions (A–J) with their corresponding definitions (1–12). Write the correct numbers in the grid below. Be careful: There are two definitions that you do not need.

A huge
B (to) raise
C awareness
D (to) profile
E race
F (to) make a point
G few
H interested (in)
I headline
J justice

1 knowing something
2 (to) describe someone or something
3 (to) give an opinion
4 a fair way of dealing with people
5 giving your attention to something you find exciting
6 words in big letters at the top of an article or a story
7 (to) send someone to prison
8 very big
9 a group of people that share a lot of the same physical qualities, like skin colour
10 a drawing
11 not many
12 (to) lift something or someone up

A	B	C	D	E	F	G	H	I	J

4 Not many

Write the correct word(s) in the gaps: a little – little, a few – few. Use some words more than once.

The bus was gone, but **1** ______________ minutes later the next bus arrived. There were **2** ______________ people on the bus, so it was easy to find a seat. An old man got on the bus too. He had very **3** ______________ money, so a nice woman paid for his ticket.

A lot of teenagers try to earn **4** ______________ extra money for things they want to buy. Fortunately, teenagers are allowed to work **5** ______________ hours in the afternoon. Unfortunately, there are **6** ______________ jobs that teenagers are allowed to do in the evening.

5 New words SB pp. 64–67

Write the missing words in the crossword.

1

3

10
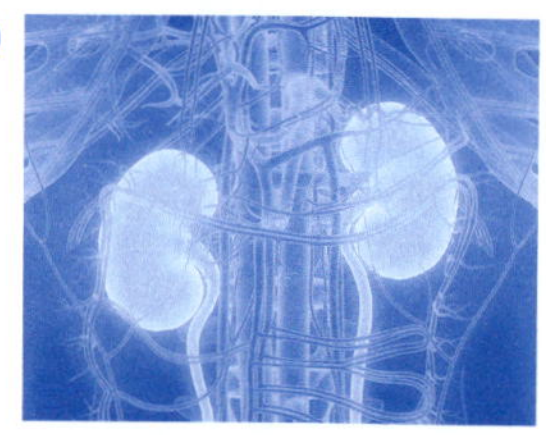

13
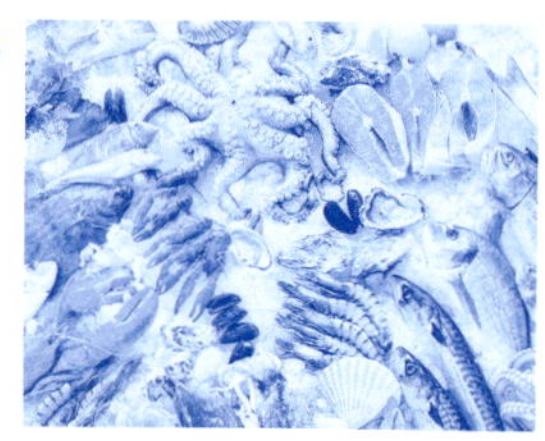

2 all the companies that produce the same things, e.g. the car ???
4 a prize you get when you have done something very well
5 You will get a ??? after you passed the exam successfully.
6 When two people fight with their hands in big leather gloves, they ???.
7 someone who does sport *(Find two words.)*
8 a book in which you collect things or make notes
9 someone who believes in what Jesus taught
11 When something hurts very badly, you are in ???.
12 If a person does something naturally well, this person has a natural ???.
14 If people bully you, it can ??? you.

6 New words SB pp. 68–70

Complete the dialogue with the words from the box.

anyway • condition • destroyed • disgusted • graduated • grew up • level • mayor • power • rebuilt • shocking • tornado

Last night we got the **1** ________________ news that a fire has **2** ________________ my grandmothers' house. It's in such bad **3** ________________ that it can't be **4** ________________.

I'm very sorry to hear that. What happened?

There was a **5** ________________ in the afternoon. The **6** ________________ of the village says it was **7** ________________ 8, which was very strong. Later the **8** ________________ was cut, so Grandma had no electricity. Some people say that she put on candles that caused the fire.

And is that true?

No, it isn't. My dad is **9** ________________. He **10** ________________ in the house and **11** ________________ from school in this village. It's his friends who say it's all Grandma's fault. **12** ________________, all we can do now is help my grandma.

7 Word families

Use the word given in capitals at the end of each line to form another word of the same word family that fits in the sentence in the same line.

1 Lots of teenagers want to raise people's ________ for the dangers of weapons.	AWARE
2 Many people are against ________ profiling.	RACE
3 A good ________ helps young people to find a good job.	EDUCATE
4 The ________ was sent to prison for life.	MURDER
5 They were ________ with burglary.	CHARGE
6 ________ went on in the USA for over 200 years.	SLAVE

8 New words SB p. 71

Complete the sentences with the words from the box.

allergy • antibiotic • appointment • documents • drugstore • pills • prescription • temperature • twice

Jaz is feeling quite ill. That's why she had an **1** ________ with her doctor this afternoon. She had taken her **2** ________ at home and it was a lot higher than it should have been.

Jaz doesn't normally take **3** ________, but now she thought she needed an **4** ________. She hoped her doctor would write a **5** ________ for it.

Jaz gave her **6** ________ to the doctor's assistant and went to the waiting room. But the doctor thought she had an **7** ________ to nuts and sent her to the **8** ________ to buy some medicine that she has to take **9** ________ a day.

9 Phrases with (to) take

Complete the sentences with the correct words. Use the pictures to help you.

1 
The nurse is *taking* ______
his ______.

2 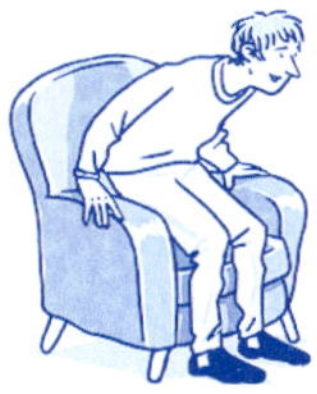
The man is *taking* ______
a ______.

3 
They are ______
______.

4 
She is ______
______.

5 
They are ______
a ______.

6 
They are ______
a ______.

7 
She is ______ his
______.

8 
They are ______
______ in a protest march.

10 New words SB p. 72

a) Write the English words on the lines.

1 
______

2 
______ (AE)
______ (BE)

3 
______

4 

______

5 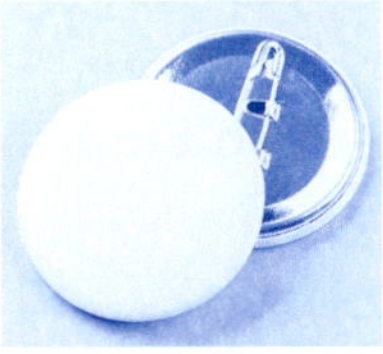
______

6 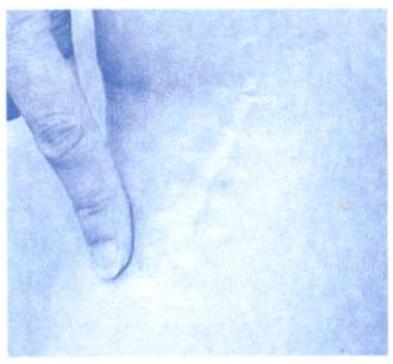
______

7 
______

8 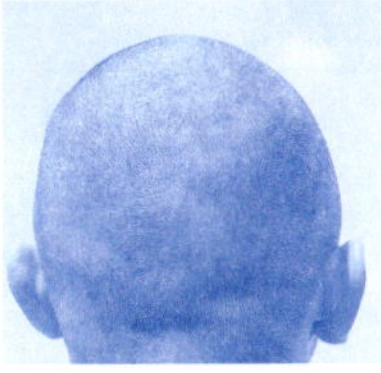
______

b) What do the following words mean? Match the expressions (A–K) with their corresponding definitions (1–11). Write the correct numbers in the grid below.

A (to) push
B title
C proof
D fool
E lip
F (to) arrest
G registration
H (to) pull sb. over
I in one's mid-thirties
J it's none of your business
K (to) pat

1 it has nothing to do with you
2 ►► stupid person
3 the outside part of your mouth
4 a piece of paper with information about a car and its owner
5 a thing that shows that something is true
6 (to) touch with your hand in a friendly way
7 being about 35 years old
8 ►► headline
9 something that only the police is allowed to do to someone who has committed a crime
10 (to) show a car driver that he/she has to drive to the side of the road
11 ◄► (to) pull

A	B	C	D	E	F	G	H	I	J	K

11 American English – British English

Write the missing words in American or British English and their German meaning.

	American English	British English	in German
1		luggage	
2	candy		
3		(school) year	
4		biscuit	
5	driver's license		
6		lift	
7		cinema	
8		timetable	

12 New words SB pp. 73–75

Write the missing words in the crossword.

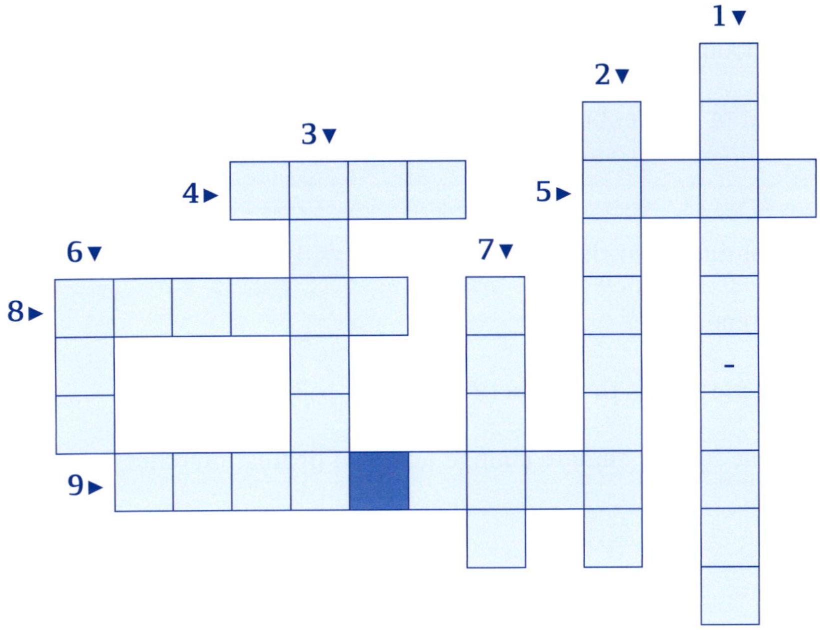

1 a comment in a film that is given by a person who isn't seen on the screen

2 what people do or say as a result of something that has happened

3 very surprised

4 the way you breathe when you are shocked or in pain

5 (to) make changes to a text or script

6 space above the earth – where the clouds are

7 (to) close and open your eyes very quickly

8 (to) shout in a loud and high voice, because you are hurt, excited or scared

9 People often ??? ??? things they don't really need. *(Find two words.)*

13 Verbs and nouns – same spelling, different pronunciation

These words have the same spelling as verb and noun, but for some of them the pronunciation is different for verb and noun. Circle these words.

access | cause | challenge | debate | experience | flood | guard | harm

increase | lock | protest | record | rent | repair | search | speed

tip | transport | volunteer | wait

14 Verbs and nouns

Read the sentences. Some verbs and nouns are in the same form. Circle these nouns and underline these verbs.

1 We usually access our drive from the main road, but at the moment access for cars is not allowed.

2 Lots of people rent their flat or house, but for some people it has become difficult to pay the rent.

3 Sue and Dave have been volunteers at the zoo for many years, but this year Sue also volunteers in a children's home.

4 Jim plays in a band and often records their practice. He also collects records.

5 Lots of young people protest against climate change and join protest marches.

My learner log

★ My three favourite words in this unit are:

____

I can …

- say what is important to me *(Write two examples.)*:

____

____

- talk about African Americans *(Write two sentences about the history of African Americans.)*:

____

____

What was difficult in Unit 4:

____

What was easy in Unit 4:

____

What I liked about Unit 4:

____

Revision: Units 3 & 4

2

1 Definitions

What do the following words mean? Match the expressions (A–J) with their corresponding definitions (1–10). Write the correct numbers in the grid below.

A	pollution	**1**	something that children play with
B	tonne	**2**	(to) make someone do what you want, usually with violence
C	(to) recognize	**3**	where you must stay when you've committed a crime
D	toy	**4**	a shop in the U.S. where you can buy medicine
E	(to) threaten	**5**	a prize that people get for something they have done very well
F	prison	**6**	a medical condition where your body reacts to specific things, e.g. things you eat or touch and you feel ill
G	award	**7**	when things are put into the environment that harm it
H	allergy	**8**	(to) know someone when you see him or her again
I	drugstore	**9**	a small case where people keep their money
J	wallet	**10**	1,000 kg

A	B	C	D	E	F	G	H	I	J

2 What are the people doing?

Complete the sentences under the pictures. Use the present progressive.

1 He's ______________ his phone.

2 She's ______________ the door.

3 They're ______________ a tree.

4 She's ______________ a picture.

3 Crossword – American English and British English

For each picture you have to find two words: the American English and the British English word. Write them in the crossword.

1▼/17►

2▼/8►

3▼/5►

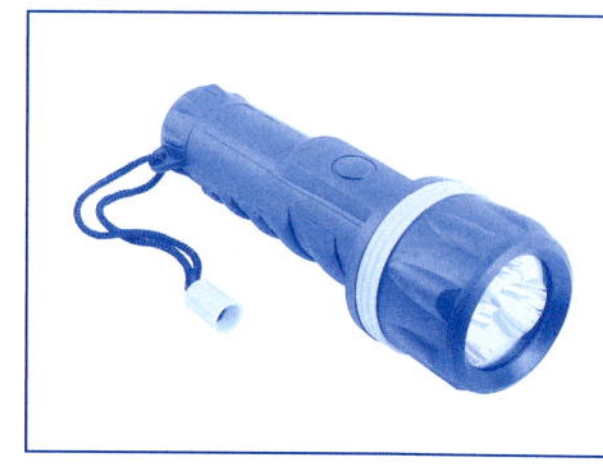

4▼/12▼

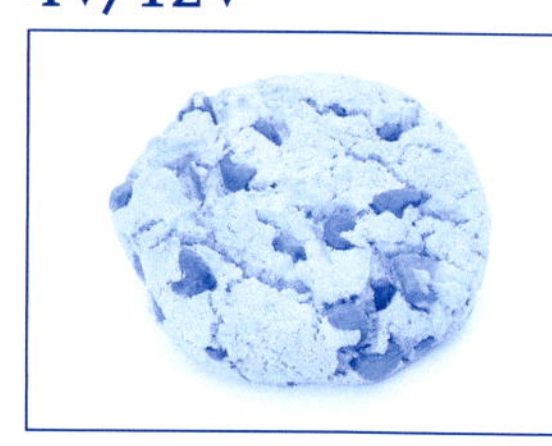

6►/13►

6▼/9►

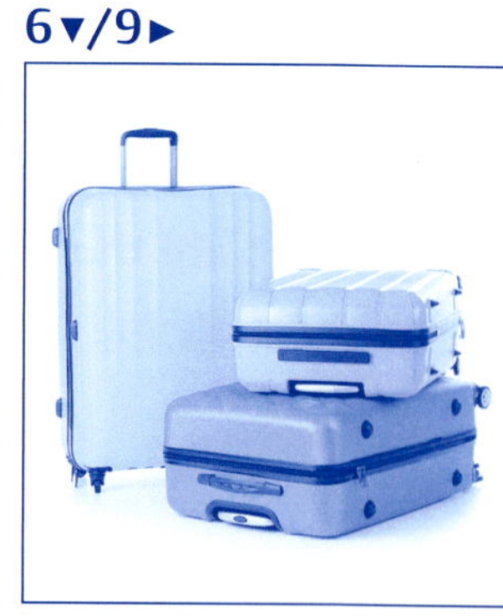

7►/ 14►

10▼/18►

11►/19►

15►/16▼

In Canada

Unit 5

1 New words SB pp. 78–79

Write the missing words in the crossword.

2

8

10

11

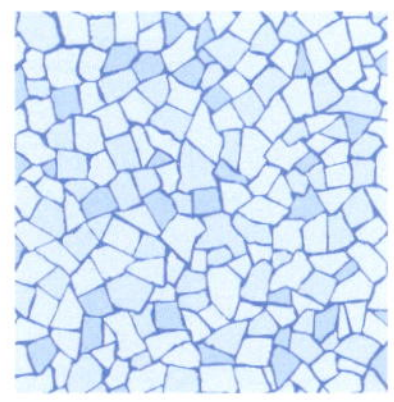

1 stress on something that is important
3 (to) dig for oil, gas, gold, etc.
4 a drawing that explains something
5 all the people who live in one country under the same government
6 a person in your family who will come after you
7 the attention from doctors and the medicine people get when they are ill *(Find two words.)*
9 a big area of land that has never been used for living or farming
12 the fact of speaking two languages
13 pictures, etc. used to make a talk easier to understand or more interesting
14 the area around the North Pole
15 a small magazine with pictures and information about something

2 New words SB p. 80

Complete the dialogue with the words from the box.

alert • Bay • fear • flashing • frightening • horns • kilos • migration • weighs • seal • sense • traps

Hi, my name is Will. I'm a member of the bear **1** ____________ team here in Churchill. We're trying to keep the bears out of town by **2** ____________ them back with gun shots in the air, car **3** ____________ or **4** ____________ lights.

Is it true that an adult polar bear **5** ____________ about 500 **6** ____________? That sounds very heavy.

Yes, you're right, and that might be one of the reasons why polar bears don't **7** ____________ people. They're big and strong animals. In the **8** ____________ months they are a real threat to people who live around the Hudson **9** ____________. That's why we're putting up these bear **10** ____________ with **11** ____________ meat inside. Polar bears have a very good **12** ____________ of smell and follow the smell of their favourite food.

3 New words SB p. 81

Use the scrambled words[1] in the box to complete the sentences.

AUMUTN • RTEIFIERD • ABBGRED • ALSCP • TITUATDE • VEHOLS • CLOAL

1 The old man had no hair, so you could see his ____________________.

2 What's your parents' ____________________ to online games? Are you allowed to play them, or do your parents think they are bad for you?

3 Last night's storm threw a tree onto our house. We were so ____________________ that we all ran out of the house quickly.

4 I want to dig a hole, but I can't find my ____________________.

5 There are four seasons: winter, spring, summer and ____________________.

6 We buy most of our food at our ____________________ shop to support the farmers in our village.

7 The little boy's father ____________________ him by his arm before he fell out of the boat.

4 Adjectives

Circle the correct word in each sentence.

Our flight to Vancouver took eleven hours. I was quite **(1) boring / bored** *in the end. My sister cried a lot – it was a bit* **(2) embarrassing / embarrassed.** *Canada's landscape is* **(3) amazing / amazed.** *Sadly, when we got to Churchill, all the polar bear bus tours were booked out. We were so* **(4) disappointing / disappointed**!
But then we were told that a bear had walked through Churchill the night before. That sounded really **(5) exciting / excited,** *so we stayed up all night and looked out of the window in our hotel room, hoping it would come again.*
Mum and Dad were **(6) surprising / surprised** *that we didn't fall asleep, but they also* **(7) worrying / worried** *that it might be* **(8) depressing / depressed** *for us not to see a bear.*

[1] scrambled word *Schüttelwort*

5 Word families

Use the word given in capitals at the end of each line to form another word of the same word family that fits in the sentence in the same line.

1 You can't buy love and ________________ with money.	HAPPY
2 When you write a text, you should ________________ your main idea so that readers know what your opinion is.	EMPHASIS
3 Children often aren't ________________ of the dangers around them.	AWARENESS
4 Lots of immigrant children are ________________.	BILINGUALISM
5 ________________ from one country to another country is nothing special these days – in fact, a lot of people do it.	MIGRATE
6 Lots of people try to lose ________________ by eating healthily.	WEIGH

6 New words SB pp. 82–83

Complete the sentences with the words from the box.

adventures • canoeing • confirm • fishing • make excuses • outdoors • suggestions

Do you like being 1 ________________ *?*

Do you like great 2 ________________ *?*

Have you ever tried 3 ________________ *?*

Or do you prefer to go 4 ________________ *?*

These are just some 5 ________________ for what you can do at our holiday resort. So, don't 6 ________________, and book your holidays with us. All you have to do is fill in the form below and 7 ________________ the booking with your signature.

7 New words SB pp. 84–85

What do the following words mean? Match the expressions (A–H) with their corresponding definitions (1–8). Write the correct numbers in the grid below.

A follow-up

B (to) mention

C general

D legend

E (to) treat

F (to) kiss

G marmot

H subtitles

1 a small European or American animal that lives in holes in the ground

2 dialogue or descriptions on the bottom of the screen for people who don't know the language spoken on the screen or for people who can't hear

3 (to) touch somebody with your lips

4 (to) behave towards somebody or something

5 (to) write or speak about something or someone without giving much emphasis, even if the information is important

6 not in detail

7 coming after something similar that came earlier

8 a story from ancient times or a famous person

A	B	C	D	E	F	G	H

8 Word families

Use the word given in capitals at the end of each line to form another word of the same word family that fits in the sentence in the same line.

1 A good ______________ will help you find an interesting job.	EDUCATE
2 In bad weather, drivers must ______________ their speed.	REDUCTION
3 The fridge was an important ______________.	INVENT
4 Doctors haven't found a ______________ for the disease yet.	TREAT
5 ______________ needs to be reduced, as it makes people ill.	POLLUTE
6 Crying isn't a sign of ______________.	WEAK

9 New words SB pp. 86–87

Read the sentences and write the words that complete them in the crossword.

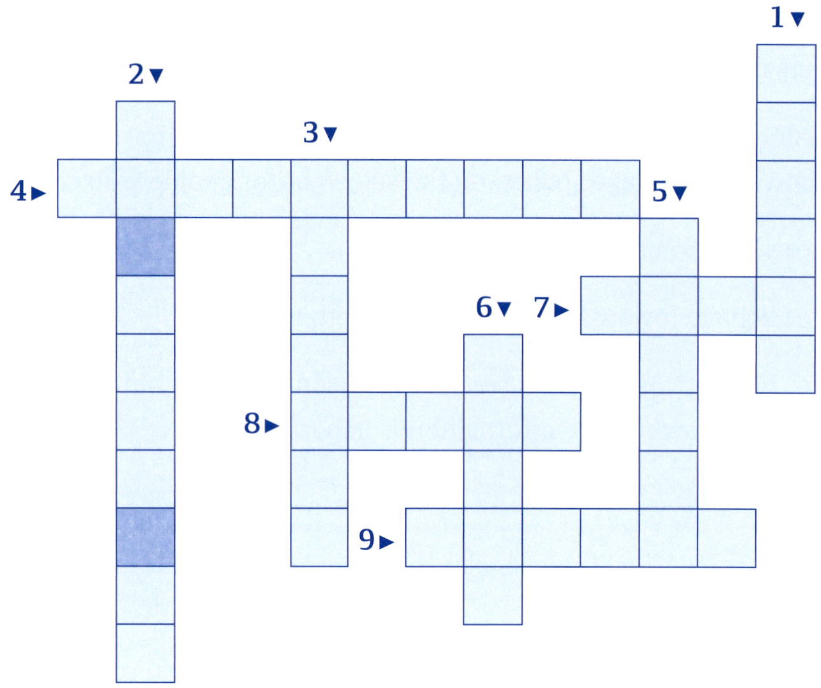

1 Riders should always wear a ??? to protect their heads.
2 Jim is working hard and saving his money. I'm sure that he will ??? buy his own horse soon. *(Find three words.)*
3 Sarah had a riding accident and was badly ???.
4 Children need their parents' ??? if they want to take riding lessons.
5 ??? racing is usually for girls. The fastest rider wins the competition.
6 There is a kind of ??? race in which each team has four members and three horses. One person has to ride all the horses.
7 After the first ??? around the track, the rider has to get on to the second horse. The rider who finishes first on the third horse wins.
8 Wild horse riding is always an important part of any ???.
9 Usually, riders put a ??? on the horse's back to sit on.

10 How to say it

*Where is the stress in the words in **bold**? Circle the part of the word that you stress when you say it.*

1 Understanding **diagrams** is an important skill.

2 Global warming threatens the lives of **polar** bears.

3 Canadians often describe their population as a **mosaic**.

4 Silvio was a school **legend**.

5 **Rodeos** are very popular in Canada and the U.S.

11 New words SB p. 88

Complete Sarah's letter with the words from the box.

buck • cruelty • Dear Sir or Madam • Finally • possible • publish • straps • Yours faithfully

1 ______________________

I'm writing to start a debate on horse riding shows in our town.
In my view, horses often experience 2 ______________ in these shows.
The tight 3 ______________ that are put around their stomachs cause them pain and make them 4 ______________ which may cause back injuries to them. It's even 5 ______________ that they die from these injuries. I understand that lots of people like these shows and believe that they are part of our culture.
However, animals should not have to feel pain for our entertainment.
6 ______________, these shows can be dangerous for people too.
Please 7 ______________ my letter in your magazine. Maybe other people share my opinion on this issue. Thank you very much.
8 ______________________
Sarah White

12 New words SB p. 89

Write the English words under the pictures and complete the sentences with the right words.

1

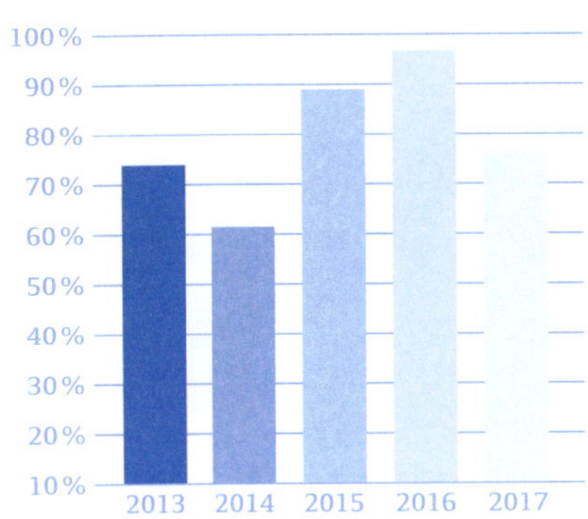

__________ ______________

2

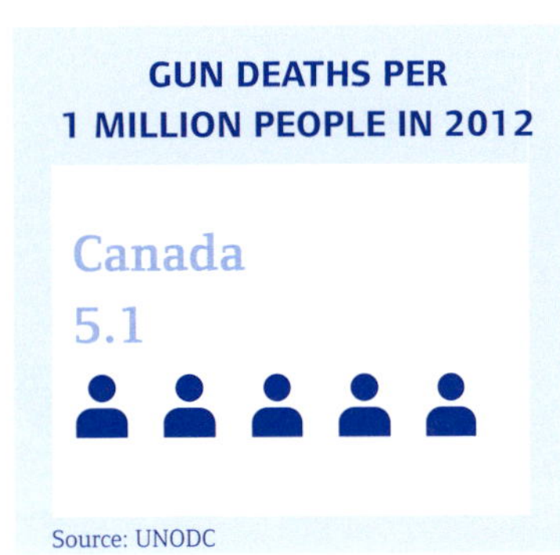

__________ ______________

3

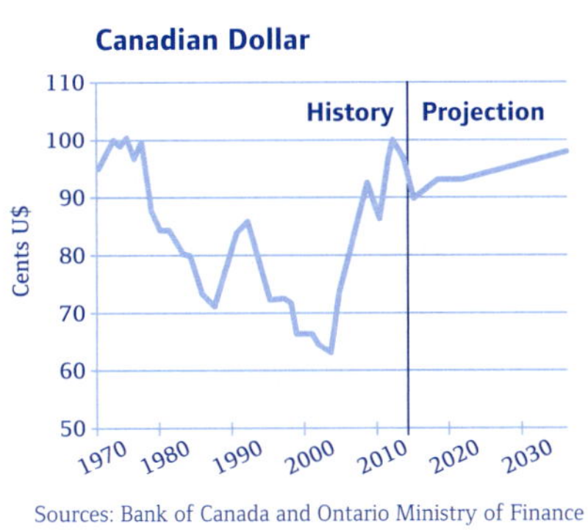

__________ ______________

The visual in number 2 shows that 4 ______________________ million people in Canada died from gun shots in 2012.

The visual in number 3 shows the 5 ______________________ of the Canadian Dollar since 1970.

13 New words SB p. 90

a) What do the following words mean? Match the expressions (A–L) with their corresponding definitions (1–12). Write the correct numbers in the grid below.

A alive
B (to) set off
C either … or
D (to) stare at
E (to) trip
F (to) reach (sb./a place)
G (to) slip
H apart
I flesh
J (to) dare
K (to) turn off
L (to) wag

1 (to) look at someone or something for a long time
2 (to) get to (sb./a place)
3 (to) leave a road to travel on another one
4 (to) catch your foot on something so that you (nearly) fall
5 (to) be brave enough to do something
6 the soft part under the skin of a person or animal
7 (to) fall on wet or icy ground
8 (to) quickly move something from side to side or up and down
9 ►► (to) leave, (to) begin a drive, walk or journey
10 these words show that two things are possible
11 ►► living, not dead
12 not together

A	B	C	D	E	F	G	H	I	J	K	L

b) Write the English words under the pictures.

1 ______________

2 ______________

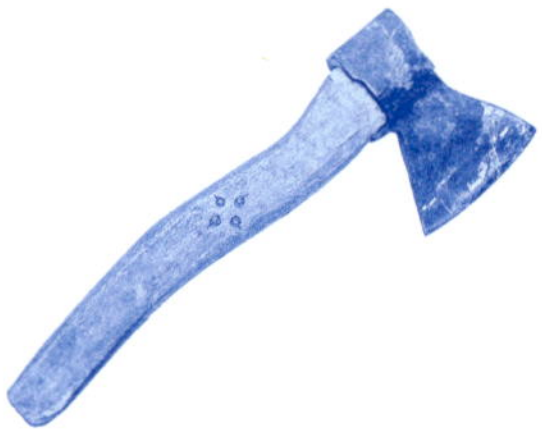
3 ______________

4 ______________

5 ______________

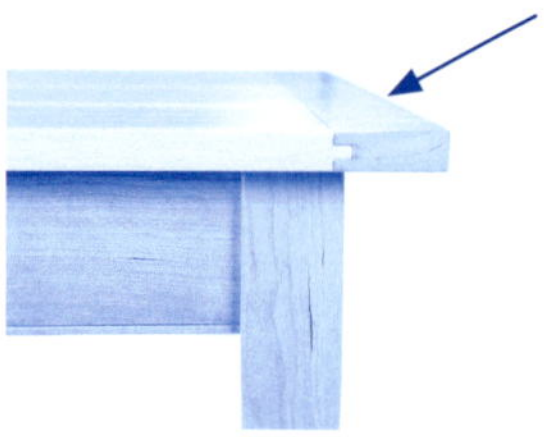
6 ______________

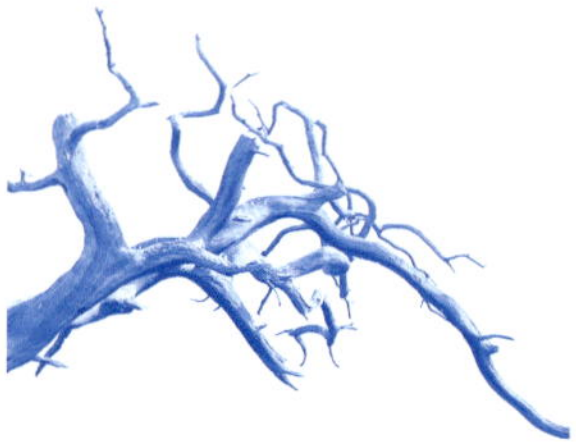
7 ______________

8 ______________

14 New words SB pp. 91–93

Write the missing words in the crossword.

3

1 (to) have something inside

2 (to) put pressure on something so that it breaks

4 the act of cutting lots of trees to make room for fields or houses

5 Everything ??? (= but not) that thing.

6 the feeling you have after pain or fear stops

8 not sure about doing something

9 what happens after you take a bite of food

11 a word that has the same meaning as another word of the same language

12 ◄► thin

13 something that you think of

7

10

15 The fourth word

Add the missing word in each line.

1	summer – winter	spring – ______
2	(to) cut – knife	(to) dig – ______
3	scalp – head	tongue – ______
4	(to) flash – light	(to) wag – ______
5	hand – finger	tree – ______
6	car – seat	horse – ______

16 Prepositions

Complete the sentences with the correct preposition.

at (2×) • by (1×) • for (4×) • from (1×) • in (2×) • to (4×)

1 Tom's brother has applied ______ a new job ______ the local hospital.

2 "Excuse me, this bike belongs ______ me!"

3 Lucy's computer hasn't been connected ______ the internet yet.

4 What year did John graduate ______ high school?

5 Car accidents increased ______ five per cent last year.

6 Point ______ the piece of meat you want to buy.

7 Jane's letter to the editor refers ______ an article she read in the magazine last week.

8 Tim has searched ______ his car keys everywhere, but he hasn't found them.

9 Teenagers who want to take part ______ online competitions need their parents' permission.

10 "Molly, please stop staring ______ the woman."

11 Everybody yearns ______ freedom.

12 "Can you reach ______ the salt, please."

13 Fifty-six ______ 100 ten-year-olds in Germany can't swim.

17 Opposites

Find the opposites.

1 ancestor ◄► ____________________

2 thick ◄► ____________________

3 together ◄► ____________________

4 either … or ◄► ____________________

5 in the beginning ◄► ____________________

My learner log

★ My three favourite words in this unit are:

____

I can …

- talk about life in Canada *(Write two sentences about what you find interesting about life in Canada.)*:

____

____

- describe visuals *(Write six words that you can use when describing visuals.)*:

____

____

What was difficult in Unit 5:

____

What was easy in Unit 5:

____

What I liked about Unit 5:

____

3 Finale

1 Compounds

*Take a word from **A** and a word from **B** to build a compound word. Add its German meaning.*

A	B
assembly • buzz • cell • civil • civil • driver's • global • health • maple • melting • natural • neighbourhood • polar • tribal	bear • care • cut • disaster • elder • leaf • license • line • phone • pot • rights • war • warming • watch

assembly line – Fließband

2 Useful objects and what you use them for

Write what you do with each object under the picture. Write sentences in the simple present.

1

I cover myself with a blanket to keep warm.

2
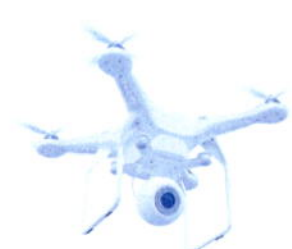

3
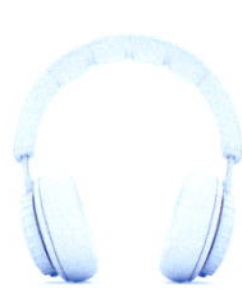

4
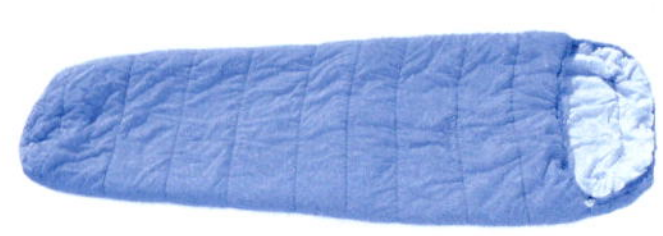

5

6
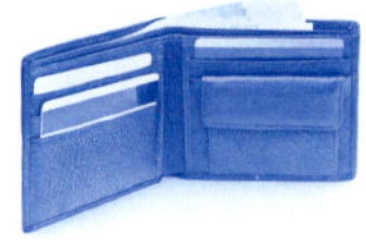

3 Who are they?

Match the descriptions on the left with the people on the right.

A the people in your family who will come after you
B the people who lived in America before the settlers arrived
C a person who brings food and drinks to your table in a restaurant
D the people who form a government
E a person you like very much, and you try to be like
F the people in your family who lived before you
G the people in the US whose ancestors lived in Africa
H a stupid person
I the head of government of a village, town or city
J a person who does a job without getting money for it

1 mayor
2 volunteer
3 African Americans
4 descendants
5 Native Americans
6 fool
7 politicians
8 role model
9 ancestors
10 waiter/waitress

4 Verbs

Circle eleven verbs in the word search (↓ ↑ → ←). Then complete the sentences with the verbs. Use them in the passive (1), gerund (2), simple past (3, 6, 7, 10), infinitive (4, 8), present perfect (5), present progressive (9).

B	E	G	I	N	A	Q
W	A	R	D	R	O	P
L	B	R	E	A	K	J
E	M	R	A	E	T	W
A	P	P	L	Y	R	O
D	L	I	U	B	E	R
S	H	O	O	T	M	G

1 The film ____________ in Canada and Alaska.

2 Most children love ____________ pictures.

3 Native Americans ____________ to make jewellery 12,000 years ago.

4 Please don't ____________ this jar. It'll ____________.

5 Luke ____________ for a new job, but he hasn't heard from them yet.

6 The polar bear attacked a tourist and ____________ off his ear.

7 Shane ____________ up in British Columbia with his grandparents.

8 Does this road ____________ to Vancouver?

9 It has been raining for weeks, so everybody ____________ for better weather now.

10 Our house had been destroyed in a fire, but we ____________ it very quickly.

5 Crossword

Write the missing words in the crossword.

1 what you feel when you are afraid
2 rivers, hills, lakes, etc. form the ??? of a country or parts of a country
3 ►► important; what you need
4 a small round hard piece of medicine
5 a piece of paper on which the doctor writes the type of medicine you need
6 what you feel when you've hurt yourself
7 the state that something is in
8 ►► 3.78 litres (in the US)
9 degrees Celsius; US: degrees ???
10 the fact that you have achieved sth.
11 ►► not many
12 what is sometimes left on the skin after an injury or operation
13 belonging to a place, e. g. ??? people
14 the state of being alone and not watched by other people
15 ►► freedom
16 a difficult task that tests sb.'s skill/ability
17 ►► side (of a lake, mountain, etc.)
18 a collection of things shown to the public, e. g. in a museum
19 the space above the earth
20 to write or speak about sth. or sb.
21 ►► not nice, really bad